O'BRIEN POCKET HISTORY OF

The Irish Famine

DR RUÁN O'DONNELL is a Senior Lecturer in the
University of Limerick History Department. He is the
author of several books on the history of Irish
Republicanism, including a two-volume biography of
Robert Emmet. He is also a board member of the Irish
Manuscripts Commission and a frequent contributor to
historical documentaries on radio and TV.

PICTURE CREDITS
The author and publisher thank the following for permission to reproduce
images:
Front cover and picture section p.8 (bottom) 'Famine' by Rowan
Gillespie, photograph © Liam Fay; used with permission.
Back cover and picture section p. 1 (top): George Frederic Watts, *The
Irish Famine*, 1850, oil on canvas, courtesy of the Watts Gallery, Surrey.
Picture section: p.1 (bottom), p.3, p.5 (top), p.6 (bottom), p.7 (both)
from the *Illustrated London News*; pp. 2 & 4, courtesy of Strokestown
House Famine Museum, Co. Roscommon; p. 5 (bottom) & p.6 (top),
courtesy of The National Library of Ireland; p 8 (top) © Eoin Fegan, used
with permission.

O'BRIEN POCKET HISTORY OF

The Irish Famine

Ruán O'Donnell

THE O'BRIEN PRESS
DUBLIN

Dedication

To the Society of Friends

First published 2008 by The O'Brien Press Ltd,
12 Terenure Road East, Rathgar, Dublin 6, Ireland.
Tel: +353 1 4923333; Fax: +353 1 4922777
E-mail: books@obrien.ie
Website: www.obrien.ie

ISBN: 978-1-84717-019-4

British Library Cataloguing-in-Publication Data
O'Donnell, Ruan
O'Brien pocket history of the Famine
1. Ireland - History - Famine, 1845-1852 I. Title II. Pocket history of the
Famine
941.5'081

1 2 3 4 5 6 7
08 09 10 11 12

Editing, typesetting, layout and design: The O'Brien Press Ltd
Printing: CPI Bookmarque, Croydon, CR0 4TD

Contents

INTRODUCTION

The Great Famine which ravaged Ireland between 1845 and 1850 was one of the most destructive episodes in modern history. The death toll, in terms of numbers and per capita impact, rivalled those endured in recent decades in Biafra, Ethiopia and Sudan. Over a million perished, one in eight of those alive at its commencement. Ireland's population never regained its pre-Famine levels and the legacy of mass excess mortality, dislocation and forced emigration did little to reconcile the survivors to the perspective of the imperial power in London. The onset of blight was natural, but many blamed the Government for its incompetent response.

The fact that the victims perished within the comparatively developed economy of the United Kingdom was shocking and has proven controversial. Many Irish, yet very few Scots, died and this imbalance posed uncomfortable questions given that the potato-dependent poor of both countries were simultaneously affected by the scourge of blight in 1845-1846. The threatened populations of the Scottish Highlands received prompt and adequate government aid to forestall the worst effects of the food shortages. It has been argued that there was sufficient food in Ireland to feed those who died from starvation and exports of livestock and cereals to Britain certainly continued throughout the crisis. Counter-famine initiatives developed by the Government ranged in quality from inadequate to partially effective. This poor, if not disastrous, performance served to highlight the absence of the national parliament abolished by the Act of Union in 1800.

Outright starvation killed huge numbers in Ireland, as did an array of diseases that were deadly to the chronically malnourished; typhus, cholera and tuberculosis wrought havoc. Social displacement exacerbated the situation when refugees flocked to the overburdened workhouses and urban centres for relief. This often fatal secondary effect was all but inevitable given the inept manner in which the country's primitive form of social welfare was administered. Disease travelled with the afflicted, whose numbers were such as to make quarantine and effective medical treatment almost impossible. There was no uniform policy governing the allocation of relief to the uprooted poor and various efforts to co-ordinate emergency measures resulted in lethal 'starvation gaps'. Such failings were, at least, unintentional. The mass evictions of the later years of Famine, however, added exposure to the common causes of excess mortality. This required specific and personal human agency; bailiffs and constables were tasked to seize goods and evict tenants by landlords availing of legislation made in Westminster. None could claim innocence of the brutal consequences of dispossession.

Death was not indiscriminate: Ireland's garrisons, constabulary, landlords, civil servants and clergy did not perish from want in 1845-1850. At least a million died because they could not afford to pay for meals, particularly those formerly reliant on the potato diet. It appeared as if the state either could not or would not keep them alive. Allegations of callousness stemmed from the knowledge that Irish produce flowed unabated to the towns and cities of industrial Britain. Theoretical debates on trade balance, market forces and inflation rates lacked credibility to those facing starvation, or, indeed to the Irish officials who urged the retention of shipments to meet urgent domestic

requirements. Anomalies of this nature have inspired the Irish Famine Genocide Committee and others to contend that London exploited a natural crisis in pursuance of strategic political objectives. Denials based on purely economic determinants have proven decidedly unconvincing. Contemporary factors, such as British concepts of 'providence', 'moralism' and '*laissez-faire*' theory, as well as base anti-Irish hostility, permit suspicion that darker forces were at work. In 1997 Britain's Labour Prime Minister Tony Blair acknowledged: 'Those who governed in London at the time failed their people through standing by while a crop failure turned into a massive human tragedy'.[1]

Recent assessments of the Irish experience during the Famine years have produced compelling insights and increasingly view the event in its appropriate international context. While the fractured and tragic history of the Great Irish Famine awaits satisfactory analysis, this book examines the key events of the period. It explores the short- and long-term causes of the Famine, local and government responses to the crisis and the impact on Irish society.

1. POPULATION

The years 1770 to 1840 witnessed a major shift in the way in which the Irish lived. Sustained population growth was the main engine of change with significant repercussions for work practices, habitation patterns and standards of accommodation. Ireland's population mushroomed from an estimated 4.75 million in 1791 to a minimum of 8.17 million recorded in the imperfect census of 1841. The limitations of this national audit meant that the real figure was probably at least 8.5 million.[2] This revealed that Ireland had the highest level of population growth in the western world. The social implications of this were considerable, particularly when coupled with the concurrent fall in death rates. Dietary improvements meant that more persons reached adulthood and advanced age than during any previous generation. Birth rates and increased longevity transformed the country which, unlike parts of England and Belgium, remained overwhelmingly rurally located. While the 1820s and 1830s witnessed a slight decline in the unusually prodigious growth rate, arising from emigration and later marriages, a demographic threshold had been surpassed.[3] The strength of this dynamic may be discerned from the fact that it occurred notwithstanding the departure to North America of 65,000 persons per year after 1831.[4]

Underinvestment by the Imperial government in London ensured that while the cities of Dublin, Cork and Belfast continued to grow in size from the 1820s, urbanisation lacked the capacity to absorb the human surplus on the land. The expansion of Guinness brewery in the capital and the healthy linen trade in Belfast concealed a general lack of industrial invigoration. Employment in Ireland's

manufacturing sector actually diminished by 15 per cent between 1821 and 1841 despite a linen-export boom centred on Antrim.[5] This overarching negative trend contrasted with the positive experience in Britain and the Continent where mechanisation and urbanisation permanently recalibrated the relationship between town and countryside. In the twenty years preceding 1841, Kerry, Clare, Galway and Mayo registered population surges in the range of 31-38 per cent with the expansion of industry in Antrim boosting its growth rate to 33 per cent. Limerick, Tipperary, Waterford, Roscommon, Leitrim, Cavan and Tyrone increased in population by 20-26 per cent. The Irish economy initially managed to withstand the pressures accruing from accentuated social distortion in the provinces. Moreover, official statistics understated the level of population growth as they pertained to the non-emigrated population and those who could be located for enumeration. Lax port administration meant that many of those who departed went uncounted.

As before, the sustained transatlantic exodus and the employment opportunities available in Britain's new cities attracted hundreds of thousands of Irish immigrants. Manchester, Birmingham, Liverpool, London and other English centres gained substantial numbers of Hibernian workers and their dependents. Yet even this productive and sustained transfer did not alleviate the mounting social and economic challenges to Irish stability. Unsurprisingly, the new pressures on Irish society created new lifestyles and contingent threats. During the period in question over five times more dwellings were built on the formerly disfavoured uplands than on the more fertile, accessible and familiar lowlands. Tangible developments had occurred by 1841 when overall habitation density on the hillsides was double that of traditional low-lying farms. A virtual

migration had taken place from the ancient farming belts into regions which had remained sparsely populated due to the marginal status of the soil, local climate and the lack of urgency in peopling such terrain. The rural poor of mid-nineteenth century Ireland were strongly in evidence on high-ground sites and throughout the barren west of the country where comparatively few had ventured in modern times. Transgressing the altitude barrier, an early manifestation of agrarian distress, occurred without significant hindrance by landlords.[6]

Potato subsistence

A major contribution to this phenomenon was the availability of the potato throughout Ireland's thirty-two counties. The potato was established in southern Munster in the late 1600s and was initially classified as a useful winter crop. The inconvenient hiatus of supply out of season was typically overcome by eating a higher proportion of green vegetables during the summer months whilst utilising potato waste to feed pigs and other livestock. From the mid-1700s the genetic adaptations of the plant to Irish conditions made it available for human consumption all year round. Animals also derived benefit from the root crop which, in the case of cattle, was reputedly an accidental discovery arising from a discarded glut proving its value in Limerick. The main strains grown in Eighteenth century Ireland were the 'Black', 'Apple' and 'Cup', although several other types were cultivated by estate gardeners for their aesthetic and novelty qualities. The 'Lumper', predominant by the early nineteenth century, had evidently been introduced to Connacht by migrant lumber workers returning from England. While the hardy Lumper strain was

intrinsically inferior to others previously sown in terms of nutrition, it answered many of the needs of small farmers across the island. The generation confronted by the Great Famine in 1845 was consequently the first in which the potato was the staple diet of the rural poor. It has been estimated that country men of working age consumed as much as fourteen pounds of potatoes a day in three equal meals. Turnip, the other significant root crop, could not rival the potato in terms of nutrition and fertility. Cabbage, also popular, was unsuitable as a mainstay of diet, but provided an important supplement.

The exponential rise of the potato occurred for many reasons. These included the increased use of the Lumper variety after 1810, which provided farmers of modest means with a highly efficient food resource. While requiring tiring spade work and some ongoing care, Lumpers maximised yields from small holdings. As much as six tonnes of potatoes could be taken from one acre of poor land. Remarkably, the strain thrived in acidic, sodden and otherwise low-grade soil, which could not sustain healthy cereals. It also acted as a highly efficient reclaiming agent and proved its utility in this regard in a country where commonage, highlands and bog were generally underused. Potato cultivation improved marginal land due to its innate biological characteristics and the ancillary practices of spreading ash and manure on 'lazy beds'. Fields were frequently dug, aerated and reseeded. Whereas arable lowland farms proved comparatively stable in terms of size and demographic profile in the mid-1800s, the clearest signs of land pressure and escalating population density were to be found in the casually regulated and more remote uplands. Whilst road building and other facets of modernisation were obviously in play, the potato played a critical role in

colonising the once sparsely-inhabited Atlantic coast of Ireland and its harsh Connacht hinterland. The potato made the agricultural exploitation of the landlocked and non-alluvial interior more viable than ever before. Those without the capital and inclination to emigrate were gifted the option of remaining on the land in Ireland.

Unlike grain, the potato did not require milling or complicated processing prior to consumption. It was easily and quickly prepared and, while no exotic seasoning was required, it benefited the inexpensive addition of salt. Potatoes were a good source of Vitamin C and scurvy was comparatively rare in Ireland. When supplemented with milk, high in Vitamin A, the basic diet of the Irish working poor was superior to most 'peasant' contemporaries in western Europe. This was particularly true of coastal counties where fish and edible seaweeds broadened the otherwise monotonous diet. Oatmeal was also commonly consumed in eastern Ulster. Travellers frequently observed that Irish people were taller and more athletic than most Europeans and this was generally attributed to the centrality of the potato in their diet. The record of the crop was overwhelmingly positive in that it did not have a reputation for unacceptable vulnerability to disease and parasitic infestation. This was not the case with more delicate cereals. The Lumper strain was so highly regarded that a critical error was made by failing to emulate the Andean practice of simultaneous planting a variety of species as a precaution against disease. This complacency was partly owing to lack of agricultural education and the estrangement of the Imperial parliament from Irish administration. It was also a testament to the strong faith in the sturdy crop. There was no persuasive evidence that a catastrophic level of

dependency had developed and certainly no sense of impending crisis in the early 1840s.[7]

Popular belief attributed the appeal of the potato to the fact that it was an underground crop for an underground people. Few decades passed in Ireland without some form of subversive challenge to the state by agrarian or political mass movements. Reasonably secure prior to digging, potato fields could be left untended at particular stages of the season and the produce stored for up to nine months after harvest. The vegetable was easily hidden in pit caches making it an ideal food supply for guerillas during times of conflict with the British and their proxies in Ireland. Potatoes were more commonly required for non-violent forms of popular resistance to authority; the sizeable illicit cottage industry of poitín distilling in nineteenth-century Ireland. Supply of ingredients was rarely problematic, notwithstanding the threat of confiscation and destruction of distillation paraphernalia by the constabulary. While it is doubtful that such factors significantly boosted the attractiveness of the crop in the early 1840s, its versatility imbued folk traditions with enduring positive connotations.[8]

Food shortages and related hardships were not unknown in the 1800s but the near total failure of a major crop was unprecedented. The terrible Famine of 1740-41 was a distant memory after the lapse of a century and its unusual characteristics offered no lessons to the descendants of those who survived.[9] There was, in any case, virtually nothing that could be done to guard against a crop-killing ice freeze. Given appropriate government management, the crop had the potential to facilitate urbanisation of a society which had been retarded by prolonged under-investment. An export business was feasible had the political will been in evidence to encourage large-scale

specialist production with appropriate road, canal and port infrastructure. This required far more expenditure and strategic planning than could be carried out by the county Grand Juries and Dublin Castle. As matters stood in the early 1840s, the gradual emergence of a dangerous over-reliance on potatoes passed without any form of state intervention.

Land and people

By the mid-1800s approximately a third of the population depended on the potato for subsistence. Many more used the crop as an important part of their diet, as was the case in mid- and eastern Ulster and the towns. Potato cultivation encouraged subdivision of farms in a country where the requirement for land reform attained chronic dimensions before it was finally addressed. The removal of sectarian legislation between 1778 and 1829 ensured that Catholics were no longer obliged to divide lands in a manner prescribed by the detested 'penal laws' but property division and alienation remained a vital concern. The rural poor could not acquire farms by purchase and consequently turned to traditional alternatives when impelled by population pressure. The plant was essential to the survival of the semi-formal co-operatives or 'clachans' which continued to proliferate on the coasts of the north-west, especially in western Ulster and Connacht. Communal farming facilitated 'rundale' holdings where labourers divided a shared allotment into non-contiguous rectangular strips.[10]

Moreover, the social tier for whom the potato was the staple food was also the least well resourced, educated and housed in Irish society. Many lived in shack-like dwellings, an impermanent and low-impact lifestyle which left

virtually no traces on the landscape. Such persons typically paid their rent by offering their labour to landlords, an arrangement which militated against the accumulation of the capital and surplus necessary for significant advancement. In Connacht and Munster this 'conacre' system often required transfers of grain, flax and hay to landlords. In general, access to marginal land, turf and potato beds was all that was necessary to start families. While emigration beyond the Atlantic and Irish Sea remained a constant feature of Irish life in the 1830s and 1840s, the rate of population growth was consistently high by international standards.[11]

'Cottiers' engaged in small scale co-operative manufacturing and, owing to this wage-earning occupation, were heavily reliant on potatoes. Those who worked outside agricultural primary production were dependent on the surplus food harvested by those who were. Paying for food was not a problem when the economy was stable, but the narrow profit margins of the cottiers left them vulnerable to inflation when potatoes became scarce. Part-time fishing was not an option for such men. Migrant labourers or 'spalpeens' were also subject to economic vagaries and eking out a living in pre-Famine Ireland and Britain was always difficult. There was a strong correlation, however, between the availability of paid work and population growth. Cottiers existed in the first instance because the Anglo-Irish economy could sustain their presence with mutual benefit and dividend. This, in turn, was predicated on the merits of potato cultivation which enabled the manufacturers to easily acquire cheap food. Fixity of place, if not also tenure, was sufficient for the cottiers to gain purchase as a distinctive subclass in rural Ireland.

'Spalpeens' played a niche role in servicing the temporary requirements of farmers for non-resident assistance during the harvest season. Prolonged absence from their native localities and families was an accepted part of the arrangement. The virtual eradication of cottiers and migrant labourers from the Irish countryside by 1850 provided retrospective proof of their precarious social position. When matters were not acute, however, the advantages of high population density were readily evident, not least in that the presence of co-operating local workers optimised yields from the labour intensive cultivation of misnamed 'lazy beds'.[12] Landlords tended to facilitate the discredited practice of subdivision as the small holders it created were self-sufficient and useful for reclaiming marginal land. They were also an immediate source of revenue and available for casual labour on the estate farms. Responsible landlords and estate managers had been discouraged from forming potentially unviable smallholdings, but the short term attractiveness of turning a blind eye to the practice proved tempting in Ireland.

The wider context for the rise of the potato utilisation in Ireland was the emergence of Britain as an advanced industrialised economy. England, in particular, lacked the agricultural primary production required to feed its newly relocated and rapidly expanding urban workforces. Consequently, Irish food and livestock exports to Britain steadily increased in volume and importance. The centralisation of political power following the Act of Union ensured that Westminster could regulate this outflow as it saw fit. Parliament had devastated the Irish textile sector in the early 1800s to protect and advantage English competitors and the House of Commons was historically disinterested in redressing economic imbalances in Ireland. Irish trade,

therefore, had a requirement for a potato-dependent underclass whose cheap labour permitted the over-production of exportable cereals, butter, beef and bacon.

In the west of Ireland, the region most dependent on potato consumption, a grim spiral of impoverisation was apparent in the early decades of the 1800s. Excessive subdivision and insecurity of tenure combined to threaten the best interests of migrants and locals. The farmed plots were simply too small and open to landlord manipulation to assure long-term stability. The environment was not only ecologically fragile but the mono-cultural exploitation of the new local economies left the inhabitants with very little room for manouevre in the face of unforeseen adversity. Furthermore, key traditional safeguards were beginning to disappear. Oatmeal, once a typical accompaniment to a potato diet, was increasingly required to fulfill rent rather than nutritional imperatives. Regional circumstances favoured the retention of the oatmeal supplement in the north east of the country, but it declined sharply elsewhere. Whereas pigs remained reasonably common and cost-effective animals, more valuable dairy cows moved beyond the reach of the poorest small farmers, along with access to their milk. For such persons, possibly as many as three million, over 90 per cent of nutritional needs were met by potatoes. They were the core of the 2.3 million people the Poor Law Commissioners reported were living in dire poverty in Ireland in 1835.

The Commissioners were by no means oblivious to the fact that an increasing proportion of the Irish nation was edging towards the precipice of disaster. However, the nature of the problem, let alone viable solutions, eluded them in the 1830s. Their viewpoint was essentially benign, but this was not shared by all commentators. Economist

Nassau Senior was quick to apportion blame where he believed it was warranted. In answer to the Third Report of the Commissioners in 1836 Senior claimed: 'I cannot admit that they are in want not from any fault of their own. If the Irish labourers allow their numbers to increase without any reference to the means of subsistence, a portion of them must every year, or at every unfavourable season, perish from want, and all of them to be in a state of permanent distress, or apprehension of distress. And as this state of things would be the necessary result of their own previous conduct, I cannot admit that it would occur without any fault of their own. The facts seem to be, that the misery of Ireland arises-I. From the subdivision of land. II. From the want of capital. III. From the insecurity of person and of property, which is the result of the two former causes ... all of them being further aggravated by improvident marriages, under which a people, a large portion of whom are every summer on the brink of starvation, are increasing in numbers more rapidly than the inhabitants of any other part of Europe'.[13]

Senior envisaged tackling this formidable 'circle of evils' by instituting 'local improvements', promoting 'emigration of the able-bodied' and administering 'relief to the impotent and sick'. Significantly, he opposed granting an Irish Board of Guardians the same power as that enjoyed by the English equivalent. Senior averred that 'the influence of party, or political, or personal feeling; sometimes the fear of Whiteboy outrages; sometimes the commands of the priest, and, still more frequently, dishonesty, would lead constantly to the grossest fraud and oppression'. For Senior the neutralisation of agrarian insurgency was an essential precursor to major land reform, after which the supposed challenges posed by Ireland's kleptocratic gentry and the recently emancipated Catholic Church could be combated.

The Great Famine soon provided an opportunity to short circuit this process.[14]

The Irish Poor Law

From 31 July 1838 the treatment of Ireland's disadvantaged inhabitants was governed by the Irish Poor Law. Legislation entitled 'An Act for the More Effectual Relief of the Destitute Poor in Ireland' arose from a long series of Royal Commissions and philanthropic investigations into the plight of the poor. Leading Irish politicians in Westminster, not least Daniel O'Connell, resolutely opposed the bill when it came before Parliament in London in 1837 on the grounds that it superimposed a rubric designed for the English economy on a markedly different social and political Irish matrix. English tenants rarely faced the problems of absentee landlords and inimical leasing practices then prevalent in Ireland. Far from relenting, Lord John Russell proposed the measure precisely because it was a derivative of the English Poor Law Amendment Act of 1834. From a utilitarian point of view it could not be denied that the Act reduced costs of regulating the lives of the English and Welsh poor while increasing social control by means of the temporary institutionalisation of 'inmates'. O'Connell and others noted that the Irish version withheld a vital aspect of the English, the statutory right to relief for all destitute persons. As in England, the workhouse was promoted as the primary agency of combating poverty, although Irish people applying for admission had no automatic entitlement to charity and could be turned away if accommodation was not available. This detail led to a range of ineffectual legislative reforms from 1845 when the daunting scale of the Irish crisis confounded the standard model applied in England.[15]

Living conditions in the workhouse were carefully engineered to ensure it was only availed of by the most desperate. Arduous and boring work was usually demanded and families divided in a prison-like institution. Even so, persons presenting themselves for entry remained subject to refusal. In the 1840s the harsh environment created for Irish entrants was sufficiently odious as to deter the type of vagrants for which the system had been devised in England. Rejected Irish applicants were theoretically prohibited from obtaining 'outdoor relief' as no such alternate provision of aid was then countenanced. One of the main advantages of workhouses, as perceived by the British Government, was that it offered an economic means to dispense with ad hoc public relief operations in times of social upheaval. In vain did opponents aver that the underemployed and underpaid Irish workers identified by the Devon Commission et al would be ineligible for entry. Whereas government level attention to minimum wage levels and reasonable terms of land tenure could have transformed the country with benefit to both distressed landlord and tenant, workhouses were inherently unproductive and regressive. Laws designed to eliminate migrant vagrancy in Britain would never succeed in tacking the structural problems of an Irish economy run from London.[16]

While the enactment of the Irish Poor Law in 1838 was a step forward, given that it was the first real effort at the national systemisation of charity, the absence of a residency requirement permitted imbalances within the workhouse network. Taxation in the form of poor rates was levied from land-holders to support their local Poor Law Unions and its workhouses. Yet persons availing of workhouses need not be residents within its administrative catchments or Union. The Irish destitute could flee their

work place and home parish, an ostensibly liberal benefit, but one which actually promoted the permanent abandonment of locality and the spread of disease by mobile refugees. To some degree, those bearing the costs of the workhouses had a vested interest in driving potential inmates into the neighbouring Union, although this did not appear to be widespread during the Famine. By contrast, the English poor were required to remain in situ for a variety of health, financial and practical issues.

Conflicting rights of movement and workhouse admission virtually guaranteed bad consequences in terms of public health and the resources of rate payers. Early tests of this novel policy were faced in 1838 and again in 1842 when short recessions created hardship across Britain and Ireland. From the outset, therefore, the Government realised that the Poor Laws were adequate for tackling endemic forms of social deprivation such as homelessness and general poverty, but were unequal to the multifaceted challenges posed by major emergencies. Allowance had to be made for occasional extraordinary, short-term expenditure, even if the Imperial writ did not entertain flexibility and expediency. The question of mid-term planning for a sustained economic crisis was left entirely open and this exposed dire administrative failings in 1846-7.

The Poor Law Commissioners for England and Wales were tasked with implementing the Irish Act. Drafting errors and the patent unsuitability of the legislation in the Irish context was revealed with alarming haste. It proved impossible to adhere to laws stipulating that the scheme be administered by means of territorial 'Unions' based upon electoral divisions made up of townlands. The gross irregularity of such zones in Ireland was without parallel in Britain and an embarrassingly early set of amendments to the

Act proved necessary. When the Famine struck in late 1845, the urgency of replacing this nominally executive body with a more responsive and informed Irish Commission became uncontestable. This only occurred in July 1847 when tens of thousands of their charges had died from starvation and related diseases. By 1841 there were 130 Unions projected for Ireland with independent Boards of Guardians. Board members were either appointed by the state authorities or annually elected from the ranks of local ratepayers and other privileged persons. They were by no means representative of the population as the traditional conservative policy of restricting the franchise and authority to those with vested financial interests in the country was once again applied to Ireland.

The majority of Irish workhouses were designed by English architect George Wilkinson who had fulfilled similar contracts in his native country. Three basic types of workhouses were built in Ireland to accommodate a maximum number of 300, 600 or 1,000 respectively. All were constructed with a view to possible expansion if a severe recession of the extremity of the 1799-1800 food shortage recurred. As in nineteenth-century prison building, boys and girls and men and women were separately housed. They had their own yards for both work and interaction in a regime intended to discourage entry and long term occupancy. Wilkinson's ambitious programme, predominately new building with some reconstruction, was advanced in April 1843 when 112 facilities were ready and the majority of the remainder neared completion. The huge sum of £1,145,800 was expended by 1847 to bring the first 130 workhouses into operation and this assumed unforeseen importance that year when the near total collapse of the Irish rural economy created acute demand. Around 115,000

persons could be simultaneously accommodated in the workhouses by early 1847 and there was built-in capacity to facilitate expansion.[17]

2. THE COMING OF BLIGHT

The immediate cause of the Great Famine was *Pyhtophthora infestans*, a fungal pathogen of unverified origin which in modern times has attacked potatoes, tomatoes and the pear melon. It struck to its greatest extent in recorded history in Ireland in the 1840s when the potato crop was repeatedly devastated and colossal loss of life ensued. 'Blight' was particularly difficult to combat; the different forms of spore transmission made it virtually impossible to detect the fungus until it was well established and untreatable. Such complex attributes ensured that the genus was not properly identified until 1876 when the German biologist Anton de Bary deduced the agency of late blight fungal infection. It was almost a century before scientists accepted that humid weather conditions, prevalent in western Europe in the mid-1840s, had merely optimised germination and wind-born contagion of the infective spores. Containment was well beyond the ability of continental farmers in the last week of June 1845 when the presence of blight was first reported in Belgium. This outbreak pointed to its probable importation via Ostend, possibly in the course of 1844. The disease spread from Flanders to northern France and the Netherlands by July 1845. Confusion was understandable given that C.F.P. von Martius and other European scientists were still debating an outbreak of dry rot or 'taint', which had attacked potatoes in the German states in 1841.[18]

Contemporary Irish, British and European biologists were unable to locate the source of the disease. Later speculation suggested that blight emanated from a Mexican genotype and became established in the eastern United

States and Canada prior to its transmission to the Low Countries. Certainly, the eastern US experienced a severe blight in 1843-4 that was well within the sphere of the Atlantic ports. This was a striking coincidence if unconnected to events on the Continent the following year. Andean origination and the role of guano trafficking have also been theorised as blight was then present in South America and could well have been spread in the cargoes of fertiliser exported to Europe. The most probable route of the first major Trans-Atlantic infection pinpoints imported North American seed potatoes. Blight rapidly contaminated a swathe of European farmland between July and September 1845 when susceptibility appeared contingent on the chance alignment of genetic, climatic and seasonal factors which promoted virulence.

Blight, an affliction without precedent in Ireland, was publicly reported on 6 September 1845 in the pages of the *Dublin Evening Post*.[19] At first it did not appear as if the scourge known to have caused severe problems in North America, the Continent and parts of England, would reach Ireland. The paper reported:

'We have made rather an ample report of a matter of great importance ... the failure of the Potato Crop – very extensively in the United States, to a great extent in Flanders and France, and to an appreciable amount in England. We have heard something of the kind in our own country – especially along the coast – but we believe that no apprehension whatever is entertained even of a partial failure of the Potato Crop in Ireland ... There may have been partial failures in some localities; but, we believe that there was never a more abundant Potato Crop in Ireland than there is at present, and none which it will be more likely to secure'.[20]

Even when the effects of blight were tentatively identified in Wexford and Waterford, there was no apprehension that the impact would be of the chronic dimensions experienced a few weeks later. However, unknown to the readers of the Dublin press, the hot and unusually wet weather experienced in July/August 1845 created the ideal environment for the propagation of the unidentified *Phythopthora infestans*. Spores may have blown across the Irish Sea from England and Wales, although the intensity of Anglo-Irish shipping and the characteristics of the disease all but guaranteed a crossing that year. By early October 1845, those *au fait* with the basic nature of the scourge in other countries were in a position to confirm its appearance in Ireland. A reassessment of an initially dismissive prognosis occurred in late October when it was realised that a considerable proportion of plants which should have been fully mature had been utterly destroyed. Significant yield reductions and temporary hardship then seemed probable but few expected a near fatal blow to the regional economy. The malignancy of blight, however, soon justified the most pessimistic forecasts.

Other countries affected by blight, such as the Netherlands, quickly reduced import taxes on food in order to compensate for losses of the domestic potato crop. This ultimately proved inadequate to ward off excess mortality caused by starvation and related illnesses, but it undoubtedly preserved thousands of Dutch lives that would otherwise have been lost. The Belgian government also intervened with comparative success while several German states either totally embargoed or limited food exports. Decisive and prompt measures required executive proactivity and could have been implemented in Ireland if deemed necessary by Westminster. Indeed, the responses

of various European administrations were positively noted in Irish newspapers in order to lobby the Government to emulate the precautions. While calls for the imposition of similar policies in Ireland and Britain were ignored, London was not totally unprepared. In October 1845 a Scientific Commission established by Prime Minister William Peel began to release statements with concrete recommendations. Professor Robert Kane of Queen's College, Cork, was a leading member of the Scientific Commission which failed to reach consensus on the precise nature of the disease. Blight was erroneously classified as a form of wet rot which seemed to corroborate observations that the disease had affected Ireland approximately two months later than other countries and with a lesser degree of virulence. Time scale and weather appeared to have considerably more relevance than was actually the case.[21]

This mistake tallied with the assertions of equally perplexed advisors of the Lord Lieutenant of Ireland, William A'Court (Baron Heytesbury). David Moore, the Scottish curator of the Botanic Gardens, Dublin, opined as early as August 1845 that unusually damp weather had stimulated a fungal disease. This conjoined two prevailing, but distinct, theories of causation. Problems in classifying 'blight' ensured that there was no agreement amongst Moore's colleagues as to whether such problems could recur in the following growth season. This attained significance in the context of possible provision of relief measures, given that a one-off affliction, fungal or otherwise, would not require ongoing major investment in famine avoidance. The judgment of Peel's Scientific Commission also had important implications for the encouragement of re-planting as it was wrongly held that Irish seed potatoes would flourish when normal weather patterns resumed. Most British and French

biologists were reassured by their own incorrect findings that the blight did not appear to be fungal in character. As the debate continued through late 1845, European governments acted with renewed urgency to control food exports. Prussia, where losses had been light in September 1845, banned exports of potatoes as a precaution. Only Peel vacillated.[22]

If the British Prime Minister genuinely discerned exaggeration in the alarming messages emanating from Ireland, his refusal to inaugurate Continental style contingencies was also in evidence. Protectionism was a controversial issue in Britain and state intervention was anathema to the vociferous Whigs in Opposition. London was very wary of opening British markets to overseas rivals and the notion of subsidising imports ran counter to economic policy. Prompt Irish appeals to place a temporary ban on potato exports from Ireland and to open the country's ports to foreign grain imports were rejected out of hand. Indeed, Irish produce was being exported to the Netherlands to increase their dwindling food supply at the very time that native stocks were reeling under the same hammer blow. The sheer multiplicity of Irish accounts reaching London by mid-October pointed to a major failure of the staple crop of millions. The seriousness of the problem varied from county to county but all, nonetheless, were affected. Within weeks of convening, Peel's three scientific advisors had reported revised productivity forecasts for Ireland that actually overstated the threat to the country's food supply. This analysis simply could not be ignored. In early November 1845 Peel made belated arrangements to secure £100,000 worth of American grain, an initiative that required secrecy lest it prove politically unpopular with the Whigs and general public.

In Tipperary, a predominately fertile and extensively farmed environment, the Boards of Guardians in a number of market towns were prompt in issuing advice to farmers on how to respond when the symptoms of blight appeared. The Royal Agricultural Improvement Society encouraged a new form of storage to increase ventilation of good potatoes that were otherwise pitted in the traditional manner. In reality, there was virtually nothing that could be done to impede let alone counter the onslaught. The category of farmers most likely to respond to well-intentioned strategies of Guardians was the least likely to suffer death. Those hampered by rudimentary education and a resultant literacy deficit in English, were ill-equipped to utilise printed recommendations circulating from Dublin and Anglophone rural towns. Peel, more than most, was capable of grasping the essential logistic issues. He had entered parliament for the borough seat of Cashel, Tipperary, in 1809 and served as Chief Secretary in Dublin Castle during the unsettled years of 1812-18. The sheer novelty of the blight ensured that this experience counted for little in the 1840s.[23]

Cultural estrangement cannot be entirely discounted as an additional force of local inhibition. While the fault lines of Irish society beyond the urban centres varied considerably in girth and depth, the public statements of landlords carried little moral weight. From the perspective of the besieged margins, a previously unknown condition had made its presence known at the same time as unconvincing advice from the infected regions. All the signs were ominous. Techniques which had failed in Waterford were known to have also failed in Tipperary. The lesser impact of the blight in Derry and Fermanagh, by the same token, could not be attributed to pre-emptive methods, or even the tenant-friendly leasing terms of the 'Ulster custom'.

Antrim remained badly hit despite the cushion of a comparatively diversified economy and the dietary benefits of the oatmeal supplement. Figures compiled by the Constabulary revealed that potato prices more than doubled in Belfast, Larne, Ballycastle and Lisburn.[24] However, it is doubtful if theories of blight containment ever held currency in the zones where the once acclaimed potato was the only real option. No alternate crop could be planted in time to compensate for the loss of the staple: season, seed and soil were immutable negative factors. With a speed deemed supernatural by some and divine by others, the juggernaut of blight assailed the subsistence economies of Ireland in late 1845.[25]

Blight destroyed potato plants by attacking foliage and infecting the tubers. Damage to leaves severely curtailed the life cycle of the vegetable and either reduced or totally aborted the tuber yield. The most visible early sign of infection was the light green spots which formed on the edges of leaves which then increased in area and darkened in colour. The spots often turned black with mildew forming on the underside of leaves around portions which had perished. In some instances the stem of the vine developed lesions that quickly killed the plant. Rotting vines emitted a powerful stench which added to the sense of dread and repulsion arising from its off-putting physical appearance. Rainfall assisted the spread of the infection by washing it from necrotic foliage and stems into the soil. This hastened the infestation of the underground tuber and poisoned the 'lazy-beds'. Potatoes often appeared normal when freshly dug from the soil only to succumb to rot in a matter of days or when placed in storage. The fact that a plant could mutate from full health to an inedible black mush in such a short interval underlined the pernicious

character of blight. Devastating crop losses occurred owing to the exceptionally high rate of contagion. *Pyhtophthora infestans* proved to be a pervasive and persistent plague. Spores traveled by wind, lingered in the ground of infected fields and survived in the fermented carcasses of blighted plants. While it was impossible to gauge in 1845 how the crop of 1846 would fare, many commentators grasped that a disaster of great magnitude was in the offing.[26]

Politics

Scientific dissension on blight strengthened the hand of those opposed to recent political developments in Ireland. Supporters of the status quo resented moves to devote state finances to a part of the United Kingdom where the primacy of Westminster was being challenged. In this respect, it is difficult to decouple many early reports of encroaching famine conditions from the larger context of Anglo-Irish friction on the Repeal question; from April 1840 O'Connell had headed the Repeal Association which pledged to restore Irish independence by means of resurrecting the national parliament at College Green. This necessitated voiding the Act of Union (1800). Mass meetings of a level rarely seen in western Europe steadily gathered momentum for the campaign until 8 October 1843 when the Government used coercion to ban a huge rally planned for Clontarf, Dublin. The imprisonment of O'Connell between May and September 1844 debilitated the most talented advocate of Irish affairs in Westminster at a time when his credibility amongst nationalists was also waning. A major dispute with the militant Young Ireland grouping had arisen over their opposition to the (Queen's) Colleges Bill of May 1845 and his repudiation of their acceptance of

political violence as a last resort. Consequently, while O'Connell retained considerable stature in the public mind, his Irish power base was seriously eroded during the early years of the Famine. Repressive legislation deployed against the Repeal Association and Young Ireland, however, ensured that Westminster's Famine policy could not be threatened by mass demonstrations in Ireland. There could be no rallies in Dublin. Anti-Repeal sentiment in Britain, moreover, had reduced O'Connell's cachet with former Whig political allies just as they prepared to challenge for Government.[27]

The Famine situation was cynically exploited by O'Connell's enemies in a bid to prejudice middle-class English opinion, the only sector of the population with political influence. This evidently motivated Thomas Campbell Foster, who commenced a purportedly fact-finding tour of Ireland on behalf of the *Times* of London in September 1845. Foster openly sympathised with the Orange Order and his ultra-loyalist views clearly informed his use of vituperative and supremacist language in relation to the majority population. Connacht's poor were depicted as 'unenterprising and unenergetic' and Foster generally castigated what he characterised as Ireland's tiresome dependency on Britain.[28] There was no factual basis for such comments, even if Foster was in a position to give eyewitness testimony. When challenged by O'Connell, Foster's secondary objective of generating anti-Repeal propaganda for *Times* readers was aggressively pursued. A visit to O'Connell's Derrynane Estate in Kerry in late September inspired damning accounts of neglected tenants, which must have encouraged those unsettled by the resurgence of pro-Repeal agitation in Tipperary. Foster's reports told British conservatives and liberal economists exactly what they

wanted to hear *vis a vis* the allegedly progressive and regressive poles of Irish society.[29]

The *canards* and half-truths of the *Times* were not calculated to improve Ireland's inadequate poor relief apparatus. Funding regulations used to finance the separate North Dublin Union and South Dublin Union had been a bone of contention prior to the Famine due to the imbalance in property values and rate-payer contributions on both sides of the River Liffey. Issues of jurisdiction and statutory responsibility became acute when the ill-effects of food shortages in rural Ireland began to exacerbate the endemic problems of metropolitan slums. In September 1845 the Poor Law Commissioners warned the city Unions to brace themselves for an influx of 'inmates' whom they expected to seek refuge in the capital. By November, the increasing scale of the disaster inspired a well intentioned strategy to promote economic recovery of workhouse residents by training them in alternate modes of utilising the potato. However, the merit of instructing people in the skills of converting potatoes into flour, pulp and starch was reliant on a rapid recovery of the crop. Encouraging renewed confidence in a staple which did not rebound was counterproductive. More desperate measures, such as classes in generating farina from diseased potatoes, proved a total failure. The process simply did not work. Having attempted to fulfill their civic duty, the Guardians of the North Dublin Union felt compelled in December 1845 to press the Government to 'open the ports for the purpose of saving the population'.[30] By then, Peel had ascertained that the Irish potato crop was approximately two-thirds its normal size. This shortfall concealed the full extent of blight damage as a bumper year had been expected owing to increased

planting in 1844 and relatively good yields had been achieved in parts of Ulster.

A major problem was posed by the fact that Britain remained an undemocratic political entity. The franchise was restricted to men of the landed and upper-middle-class tier of society and the quest for 'one man one vote' did not reach fruition until the twentieth century. The aristocratic House of Lords retained an absolute veto of any legislation presented by the narrowly elected House of Commons in the 1800s. The views of ordinary Britons, moreover, counted for little and organisations which articulated their perspectives were subject to vigorous repression when the Government felt threatened. The reasonable demands of Chartism were coerced into oblivion as recently as the 1830s and Parliament was even more forthright in derailing O'Connell's Repeal crusade in 1843-4. John Frost and other militant Chartist leaders in England faced transportation to Van Diemen's Land in 1839 where several leading Irish radicals were actually sent in 1848-9.[31] Far from leading the enlightened world, England lagged behind the supposedly despotic Napoleonic France of the 1810s in the fields of political, educational and legal entitlements. Westminster had only abolished slavery in 1833 and, having indemnified its discommoded profiteers to the tune of £22 million, assisted the Confederacy during the American Civil War in the early 1860s.

The emancipation of non-conformist Protestants in 1828, followed by that of Roman Catholics in 1829, extended rights to many once deprived, but Britain was not remotely democratic prior to 1918. The emancipation deal foisted on O'Connell's followers in 1829 actually reduced the voting population by means of raising the property qualification for the franchise. With no broad voting base

and no popular press to harness public opinion, Westminster was virtually impervious to electoral pressure during the Famine. Ireland had been deprived of its national political forum on 1 January 1801 and dispatched MPs and Peers to London where the interests of the vast majority of their constituents rarely prevailed over English majoritarianism and conservative vetoes.[32]

The Irish contingent in London, riven by disagreement on the Repeal issue and still further between vying O'Connellite and Young Ireland factions, lacked an authoritative voice to compensate for their low numbers. With William Gregory, Lord Palmerston, Earl Clanricarde and other Irish parliamentarians siding with the Government in pursuance of measures which militated against effective Famine relief, the impotence of those who followed the constitutional path to social and national justice was cruelly exposed. By 1850 Irish politicians could reflect on the fact that their pre-Famine electorate of just 122,000 men had been reduced to a mere 45,000. The subsequent haemorrhage of emigration wreaked further havoc on the body politic of Ireland and encouraged the re-emergence of the physical force alternative.[33]

Nationalists discerned opportunities to criticise the Government's handling of the crisis and did so with alacrity in late 1845. However, their efforts to receive a hearing in Westminster were primarily stimulated by humanitarian concerns. O'Connell made a series of moderate proposals to Government in late October 1845 which he claimed would radically improve the situation in Ireland. Recommendations included a scheme to employ thousands of men in railway construction, which had commenced on a major scale around the country. The largest Viking graveyard outside Scandinavia was being desecrated in the early 1840s to build Kingsbridge (now Heuston) Station. The rail

system required land clearance and track-laying, as well as the more skilled tasks of building bridges, tunnels, culverts and stations. However, it was held in London that the employment of the poor would deflate wages and discourage professional labourers and masons from executing their contracts. Dublin Corporation was told by O'Connell that absentee landlords should be taxed at 50 per cent and residents at just 10 per cent, but few believed any such reform would ever be enacted by the veto wielding House of Lords. O'Connell could only seek to persuade those with authority and, in this instance, failed to impress. Few could deny that non-resident landlords had tolerated, if not encouraged, modes of farm administration that fell well short of acceptable standards. However, the obvious correlation between landlord neglect and lack of economic improvement in Ireland was not an issue with which Peel, a man of ambition, wished to grapple in 1845.[34]

A more realistic attitude could be discerned in O'Connell's disavowal of a rent strike or total ban on food exports. Others had urged such courses of action, but O'Connell knew that a regime which had faced down his Repeal Association would not baulk at protecting the interests of Irish political allies should their income be imperiled. Indeed, the Kerryman would not press for action liable to damage the emergent Catholic middle-class professionals of which he was the most famous contemporary success story. Similarly, he appreciated that Westminster would never sacrifice English requirements for Irish produce in order to shore up a faltering national economic system they claimed to deplore. Instead, O'Connell advocated halting food exports to countries other than Britain and placing a moratorium on brewing and distillation. This compromise would immediately augment the edible grain supply in

Ireland and act as a brake on price inflation. Good yields had been achieved for the 1845 oat harvest and much of this additional surplus was leaving the country for foreign ports without being offered to the receptive domestic market. Oatmeal prices actually fell slightly in Meath in December 1845 while the prices demanded for potatoes increased.[35]

O'Connell also co-operated with Valentine Lawless (Lord Cloncurry) and Augustus Frederick Fitzgerald (Duke of Leinster) in the Mansion House Committee. It first assembled after a public gathering on 31 October and issued resolutions to Heytesbury on 5 November 1845. O'Connell and Cloncurry had secretly commenced political life as members of the revolutionary United Irishmen in 1798, but were convinced, constitutional moderates by the 1840s. The dialogue initiated by the Committee involved Cloncurry in exchanges with Heytesbury and Peel. Cloncurry argued that £1.5 million should be invested by London in the form of a loan to lower food prices. This, in tandem with the opening of state-run granaries, would feed persons with limited resources as well as the destitute. More controversially, Cloncurry and O'Connell hoped that the Government would permit the importation of corn and effectively subsidise its sale price by waiving customs duties. In this they found an ally in Heytesbury, Viceroy since July 1844, who also proved amenable to their argument for a distillation ban. Yet, grain imports necessitated either the suspension or the outright repeal of the Corn Laws, a nettle which Peel had long planned to grasp and had at last seriously considered in 1842. In this respect, the somewhat impertinent Dublin resolutions proved opportune. With some misgivings and subterfuge, Peel acted to procure American grain in the second week of November.[36]

3. INDIAN CORN, 1845-46

Prime Minister Peel ultimately authorised the purchase of £100,000 worth of maize in two consignments, which were distributed to official stores between February and June 1846. Quantities of oatmeal and maize were also quietly acquired in Britain with a total minimum cost to the Exchequer of £185,000 in food relief to Ireland by August 1846. The maize was popularly known as 'Indian corn' but also referred to as 'Peel's Brimstone', a dismissive term inspired by its supposed resemblance to sulphur and noxious consistency when cooked.[37] Maize was distributed to over 600 authorised committees around the country by a Relief Commission established on 18 November 1845. Its leading figure was Sir Randolph Routh of the Army Commissariat whose associates charged the recipients cost price for maize in order to protect the national food market from the Government's interference in the economy. Local committees, supported in theory by landlords and a matching funds grant of £68,000 from the Lord Lieutenant, resold the maize directly to those capable of paying one penny per pound. In dire cases the maize was sold at less than cost price or distributed free from special 'sub-depots'. Yet the Government was extremely wary of engaging in charity, leading Routh to comment that the imports handled by his staff provided 'almost only a mouthful' to those in need. Routh's candour was not appreciated.[38]

While official food depots were subject to a degree of regulation, the prevailing economic climate of limited supply and strong demand ensured that Routh's staff frequently failed to reach the intended end consumer. Committees had no effective mandate to channel the food to the

most desperate and chance factors, such as regional infrastructure, often dictated the siting of depots. The Connacht
seaboard was in obvious need of additional depots, but the
sheer remoteness of the population from existing transport
routes militated against state provision. Temporary respite
was the objective and one of the main potential benefits of
depressing food prices was facilitating those with some
capital to obtain affordable food. Subsidised depots had a
finite quantity of product and rigid price structure whereas
the private merchants who acquired the vast bulk of the
general imports were impeded by nothing more than commercial forces. This was perfectly legal, if unhelpful. John
William Ponsonby (4th Earl Bessborough), Irishman and
Whig appointed successor to Heytesbury as Viceroy,
informed Peel that profits of 50 per cent were being made
by speculating middlemen. Approximately six times more
maize was imported and sold by private investors than distributed for sale by the Government in 1846. This public/
private imbalance ensured that the Government imports
could not greatly curtail inflation in the national market,
particularly when most of its maize was released over just
two months. Yet demand for the official depot stocks was
extremely high and it was fully allocated in June 1846. All
Government reserves had been exhausted by August.

People who were normally suspicious of unfamiliar
food were compelled to buy maize through fear of starvation. Maize imports jumped from just seven tonnes in 1845
to 122,000 tonnes in 1846 and peaked in 1847 at a massive
632,000 tonnes. Those with savings and good wages could
buy corn throughout the 'Famine'. Unprocessed whole
maize grain required milling to produce the edible form of
corn meal and most Irish consumers, particularly those
once reliant on potatoes, were unaccustomed to this

practice. They were often geographically remote from the central stores where the maize was sold, as well as from the mills whose services then proved necessary. Corn meal required a more complicated cooking preparation than potatoes and was comparatively lacking in bulk and nutrition. Prolonged soaking and boiling could render the grain edible but this required fuel, constant attention and patience. Although maize was reputedly difficult to digest, this belief probably owed something to difficulties of preparing meals properly. The food could not be consumed raw without severe consequences. In some instances, it is evident that the corn meal distributed was unfit for human consumption and several people allegedly died from food poisoning in Waterford workhouse.

Notwithstanding such negative factors, the maize importations represented a clear cut public relations success for Peel. His imperfect intervention in late 1845 almost certainly saved lives in the course of the following spring and proved that the British Executive was cogniscent of its ability to ward off famine with targeted investment. Even so, selling maize to persons who generally subsisted by means of their own primary production had leached precious cash out of the social margins. Those threatened with famine were forced to sell their few tradeable possessions, generally livestock. Pigs were also sold or eaten, by 1846, as it proved more and more difficult to feed them anything that humans did not also covet as a meal. Given this urgent mass offloading of assets and the manner in which the small quantity of heavily subsidised maize was dumped into the food supply, it is clear that 'Indian Corn' enterprise was by no means a triumph of Tory paternalism.

The recurrence of crop failure in the summer of 1846 made it virtually impossible for those who had previously

liquidised assets to recover financially. Such reverses would have lessened the practical value of importing cheap food in a second year of Famine as those who most in need of sustenance simply could not acquire it by purchase over the winter. Unsurprisingly, banks withheld credit from the destitute in nineteenth-century Ireland. More seriously, wages continued to fall as the price of food continued to rise. Cottiers and others who worked for cash were badly hit by the increases. Heystesbury was informed of this invidious trend by Galway petitioners in April 1846 and, in the final analysis, underpayment and underemployment joined 'blight' as indirect causes of death in 'Famine' Ireland.[39] Lack of employment was constantly stressed by Medical Superintendents as a key factor in protecting the health of the country as they understood all too well the correlation between low wages, starvation and disease. By the winter of 1846-7 free, rather than subsidised, corn meal, was absolutely necessary to ward off mass starvation. If Peel's primary motivation in 1845-6 was to use maize to dampen overall food price inflation in Ireland, his successors in Downing Street did not share this concern. The rise of an implacable Whig administration under John Russell in June 1846 ensured that even this paltry option was taken off the agenda.[40]

Public works

The stratagem of using public works to provide a form of aid was applied in the early months of 1846 under the Labour Rate Act. Edward Lucas, Chairman of the Commission of Inquiry into the Famine, advised this course in February 1846. The Board of Works in Dublin, a comparatively new organisation, initiated and managed various types of

labour intensive 'outdoor relief' schemes. This represented the second strand of Peel's counter-Famine initiative, a policy which would preserve the separate 'indoor relief' system of the Poor Law from being swamped with starving refugees and the additional costs this entailed. While work on rail construction remained off-limits, the Government intended that the Grand Juries which managed county-level administration and the evolving Board of Works would provide special additional paid employment. Men and women earning wages for labouring on capital construction projects would be able to support themselves while developing national infrastructure. However, technical aspects of the funding model for such projects favoured those proposed by the Board of Works and this influenced the type and location of work carried out. Bureaucratic complexities also slowed implementation of plans, as did both real and alleged cases of corruption. Public works, as with Indian Corn, were envisaged as temporary, partial solutions to an aberrant hiatus in normal practices. They would cease on 15 August 1846 when the anticipated recovery of the potato crop should have rendered them unnecessary. Circumstances dictated that the projects continued well into 'Black '47'.

Road improvement became the main stay of public works even though the Government realised that the finances it had committed were not always spent in the districts most in need of the schemes. Projects of major regional utility, such as pier and dock building on the west coast, did not materialise. Moreover, serious problems arose in the selection of work forces, a role earmarked for the local Relief Committees, but open to abuse due to lack of supervision. If far from well-paid by general standards, the wages on public works were sufficiently high as to

compete with those of the poorer agricultural labourers. Such men were not necessarily entitled to the 'tickets' which permitted Labour Rate employment. Naturally, the lack of regulation quickly led to exploitation of the schemes by those seeking daily wages. An attempt to discourage malingering by linking payment to task completion proved unworkable, not least in that the shortage of pay clerks exacerbated the problem of prompt compensation. In October 1846 the case of Denis McKennedy became notorious when a Cork coroner confirmed he had starved to death in Skibbereen when owed two weeks wages by the Board of Works.[41]

This was not an isolated incident. John Driscoll finished work on a Bantry area scheme two months later, but collapsed 'for want of food', and was found dead in the mountain of Glounlough on the following morning. His wife proved that he had eaten nothing for two days previous to his death, except a small quantity of boiled wheat, and that he frequently had a similar fast'. The magnitude of the relief challenge overwhelmed those charged with promoting public works as a solution. Nonetheless, if properly administered and financed, public works was a potentially ideal counter-Famine initiative.[42]

In June 1846 around 21,000 were employed in public works compared with 98,000 by August. All in all, the plan of public works backed by Peel in March 1846 provided approximately 140,000 with employment on road building and other construction sites. Many workers used their pay to support dependents and the secondary beneficiaries of the schemes were consequently very considerable. Most projects came under the Board of Works but Grand Jury presentments, a forum dominated by landlords, also boosted the figures. The numbers rose sharply to 500,000

by December 1846 as a harsh winter set in, and still further to 734,000 in March 1847 when starvation killed thousands.[43]

The early schemes were heavily concentrated in Munster and Connaught with Clare and Limerick receiving 26 per cent and 15 per cent of the contracts respectively in 1846. All seven counties in which public works were then carried out had been badly hit by the Famine, although the worst affected sectors in the south and north-west of the country were not represented. This was partly due to the difficulty in matching viable schemes with poverty black spots. Sir John McNeill had advised Lucas and the Commission of Inquiry that the 'benefit of employment in public works extends at five miles only'. This radius offered a life line to those within the catchment and nothing whatsoever to those beyond.[44] Red tape was also a major problem; Irish civil servants simply could not respond with effect when Westminster suddenly devolved administrative responsibility along with a set of unwieldy legal parameters. By 1847 projects of varying degrees of practicality sprang up around the country on an ad hoc basis and the numbers employed mushroomed. Despite valid criticisms of the endeavour, the public works of 1846 were widely viewed as successful wherever they had operated. At Peel's behest, Treasury funds had been expended in Ireland in a bid to minimise the impact of the food shortage crisis.

Fitzgerald, Duke of Leinster and head of the Royal Agricultural Society, attempted to convince the Viceroy to use the cash provided for 'works of a useful and profitable nature'. Russell, then Prime Minister, responded directly to Fitzgerald from Downing Street on 17 October 1846 arguing that public works were initiated in order to employ only the 'surplus labour' Irish landlords could not utilise on their

own estates. Russell acknowledged that the function of Labour Rate Act had deviated or 'turned' but demonstrated unsettling ignorance by professing that the Scottish land-lords had overcome 'as severe a calamity, as it has been in Ireland'. A cursory glance at the Times of London would have shown the utter fallacy of this statement, a paper which averred: 'There are times when something like harshness is the greatest humanity'.[45] However misin-formed on Scotland and Ireland, Russell's displeasure at Irish landlords was significant in the context of discussions of rate levies, estate encumbrance and general Poor Law policy. Russell was by no means satisfied with the perform-ance of Fitzgerald's Society and may well have lost his patience with another member, Robert Kane, one of the sci-entists who erred in the identification of phytophthora infestans.[46]

A second year of Famine, 1846, confounded optimists in two major ways. In the first instance, blight not only reap-peared, but did so earlier in the season and in a more severe form than before. The spores were widely dispersed and well established. Every county was badly affected and corn yields were also disappointing. A second factor was that the relief response was markedly inferior to that of 1845. From mid-July 1846 it was apparent that a very destructive infestation of the potato crop had occurred and this quickly assumed the proportions of near total failure. Yet direct provision of subsidised grain had been taken off the agenda so that affordable food would not be sold to the poor out of Government-run depots. This imposed the main brunt of amelioration on the cumbersome bureauc-racy of public works. Moreover, there were disturbing signs that the physical and psychological privations endured by the poor had undermined future agricultural output. It was

ascertained that less acreage had been planted with seed potatoes for the 1846 season. Some the precious seed potato stock had been consumed, although it was also clear that many could not or would not replant for the next season. While this was only 12 per cent less than normal in Wicklow, where 14,900 acres were dug, the shortfall was indicative of a renewed sense of unease.[47]

In retrospect the productivity loss, whether arising from excessive caution, diversion of labour to public works or conservation of energy by the impoverished, was grimly prescient. Sufficient acreage had been planted in 1845 to feed the national population if the crop had been healthy when dug in 1846. Faith in this scenario had been encouraged by the official classification of the problem as an aberrant attack of wet rot, as well as widespread ill-conceived confidence that catastrophe would not follow from crisis. In July 1846 it was known that this judgement was fatally misplaced. Very little of the potato crop was edible anywhere in Ireland in the winter of 1846-7 and the threat of mass excess mortality from starvation became a reality. Lightning had confounded the scientists and civil servants by striking twice. This, in turn, had a major impact on planting for the 1847 season.

The medical authorities monitored the first phase of the Famine with a view to assessing likely trends in public health. From Markethill, Armagh, Dr. Joshua Lynn reported in February 1846 that 'fever, diarrhea and dyspepsia have increased considerably, and are in many cases traceable to the use of unsound potatoes. It is very probable that fever will break out and spread'. In Swanlinbar, County Cavan, Winslow Finlay noted 'several cases of typhus fever … insufficiency of food the cause in some instances. Fever will break out to a frightful extent in the event of scarcity of

food'. Dr. R.M. Taggard, similarly, sent details from Donaghmore, County Donegal, of outbreaks of influenza, scarlatina and small-pox. He feared 'the spread of disease, particularly fever; provisions being likely to be dear and scarce, and the supply of fuel scanty'. Health practitioners, therefore, predicted a range of serious challenges to the population if blight recurred in the 1846-7 season. All parts of Ireland were regarded as vulnerable unless the food supply, employment and anti-fever initiatives were significantly boosted.[48]

4. TORIES AND WHIGS IN WESTMINSTER, 1846

The onset of Famine coincided with a period of political instability in London as Peel and Russell vied for authority over matters arising from the internal affairs of Britain. The repeal of the Corn Laws, an issue with Irish ramifications, proved a major bone of contention. Worsening English economic conditions, the Irish situation and the determination of Peel's inner coterie to press for reform of import duties on grain combined to bring the issue to the fore. Having failed to force repeal legislation through Westminster, Peel attempted to resign on 5 December 1845 only to resume the leadership when Russell found it impossible to form a Whig government. Peel succeeded in securing the vote he required on 26 June 1846 and vacated his office in Downing Street once again. Eventual victory on the Corn Laws had been followed by defeat on an Irish Coercion Bill, much to the pleasure of the O'Connellite MPs. They and others believed that the forces of law and order in Ireland did not require additional powers to control the country. The Whigs assumed Government under Russell who became Prime Minister on 30 June and tried to impose his will on a seriously factionalised party. Functional unanimity existed on one basic point, the necessity of steering a different economic course to that of the discredited Tories. The fall-out from this inter-party struggle in England was mass starvation in Ireland. Ironically, the vagaries of policy implementation on grain imports meant that customs were still being levied in Ireland in 1847 when the Famine was at its height.

The rise of the Whigs was initially welcomed by many Irish MPs. In what appeared to be a considered move, Russell installed Earl Bessborough as Lord Lieutenant in the Phoenix Park. The Kilkenny magnate had the dubious distinction of being one the first Irish incumbents of the office and it was hoped that his national affinity would enable him to prevail where Heytesbury had abjectly failed. Bessborough was a member of a distinguished political family, the Ponsonbys, and enjoyed a good working relationship with O'Connell, which had facilitated the Kerryman's entry to the House of Commons in 1830. Expectations that an Irish Viceroy might press the nation's case in London proved illusory and Bessborough's ineffectual and frustrating tenure came to an abrupt halt when he died on 16 May 1847. While it was not altogether surprising that the holder of a largely symbolic position lacked executive influence, the manner in which the Russell administration ran its Irish affairs was far from typical. To a large extent, this responsibility devolved on two men: Sir Charles Wood, Chancellor of the Exchequer, and Charles Edward Trevelyan, Assistant Secretary of the Treasury.

Wood and Treveylan were highly regarded Whigs and ideological supporters of the party's *laissez-faire* theory. Wood was promoted out of the Admiralty by Russell in 1846 to bolster Liberal economic values at the heart of the financial administration of the United Kingdom. While unaccustomed to such power, Wood was closely advised by Trevelyan, a Treasury subordinate who had years of administrative experience in India prior to establishing his credentials in state finance in 1838. Wood's commitment to applying laissez-faire principles was immeasurably strengthened by Trevelyan's iron grip on the Treasury. Essentially, the English triumvirate of Russell, Wood and

Trevelyan believed that the state should play a minimal role in regulating the economy on the grounds that it inhibited private enterprise and ultimately weakened the country. Keeping taxation low to encourage entrepreneurs not only militated against general expenditure, but also specifically discouraged spending on schemes deemed to threaten the operation of commercial market forces. The Whigs, therefore, required low taxation and were committed to reducing Government spending. They believed that the Treasury should not interfere in the Irish economy on the grounds that this amounted to state subvention of a type that would engender a culture of dependency. In short, they argued that it was better to withhold aid so as to stimulate the type of grass roots reform that would redress the causes of failure and stagnation. Whereas traditional Toryism contained an element of paternalistic oversight, the sterile polemics of Liberal economic policy were free of any such sentimentality.

Wood studied Malthusian theories of population dynamics that held that unsustainably large communities would rebalance by means of internal migration and emigration. Yet Thomas Malthus was not particularly interested in Ireland which, contrary to popular belief, did not possess the population density as high as many European states. It is unclear if Wood subscribed to the quasi-genocidal techniques recommended by Malthus in 1826 to administrations faced with overpopulation. He suggested that they should 'facilitate' the 'operations of nature in producing this mortality … and if we dread the frequent visitation of the horrid form of famine' pursue 'other 'forms of destruction'. These included 'plague' engineered by means of urban planning, an option with more relevance to 1840s Manchester than County Meath.[49] Ireland, as both Malthus and

Wood appreciated, had a completely different social structure to that of industrial England and this circumstance lay at the heart of the perceived problem. Wood may well have reflected on the fact that he was in a key position of economic influence when 'nature', 'famine' and 'plague' co-existed to its greatest ever extent in Ireland.

The prevalence of such views in the Executive was significant but when coupled with contemporary arguments linking the causes of Famine to such subjective factors as 'Providence', 'indolence' and agricultural backwardness, the scope for justifying otherwise reprehensible inaction was enhanced. It was widely held in the upper echelons of British government that the Irish economy required radical improvement and, if the disasters visited upon it were not at least party self-incurred by archaic farming practices, the crisis presented a perfect opportunity to address a perennial problem. Irish landlords were rightly deemed highly culpable, although it ultimately proved impossible to convert the propertied classes to modern practices without dislocating their tenantry. Wood and Trevelyan grasped that mass excess mortality, migration and emigration would enable London to impose an English agricultural format on Ireland. While the two men certainly did not foster incipient Famine conditions, their response to its manifestation was utterly incompetent by contemporary national and international standards. No genocidal conspiracy was necessary to herald the destruction of the elements of the Irish economy deemed outmoded by the Government.[50]

Backed by a receptive Whig administration, Trevelyan took the extraordinary step of cancelling an order placed by Peel's Government for a third shipload of American maize. This appeared utterly callous in retrospect, particularly as it occurred after reliable early warnings had been

received which indicated that the Irish potato crop of 1846 was not blight-free. The most positive interpretation of Trevelyan's actions was that it was based on a sincere conviction that economic recovery was in prospect and that it was better for the Irish poor to revert to their habits of industry than grow accustomed to state assistance. If present, Trevelyan's optimism was cruelly misplaced and his professional competency, if in no other way remiss, was adversely influenced by a dangerous insouciance towards Irish mortality. Scotland was a different matter and Trevelyan ensured that its food depots were prioritised in 1846 despite the fact that the Highland potato crop suffered a less malignant attack of blight than present in Ireland. Discrimination was justified on the grounds that the Scots, landlord and tenant, were considerably more industrious than their Irish cousins. In truth, mass excess mortality in Scotland, or any other part of Britain, was politically unacceptable. It may not have been irrelevant that the Scots had seemingly shrived themselves of revolutionary and disruptive tendencies. Overall, the decisions of the Treasury under Trevelyan's tenure were not only erratic and capricious, but seemed to lack the most fundamental appreciation of the nature of the Famine in Ireland.[51]

While it might have been reasonably argued that the Irish poor could not afford further imports of subsidised maize, this factor was not central to the discussions in Whitehall. Instead, the maize was cancelled in a bid to force the Irish to pay market rates for local produce which had proved beyond their means at the beginning of the subsistence threat. They would also be obliged to pay for private imports of maize which rose to 632,000 tonnes in 1847 before falling back to 306,000 tonnes in 1848. This increase, added to the marked reduction of Irish grain exports in the

same period, temporarily boosted the national commercial food supply but not in time or in a manner capable of preventing starvation.[52] There was no redundancy in the Whig strategy and it was not deemed prudent to stockpile the previously contracted maize as a contingency for relief in the 1846-7 season.

Incredibly, for a man credited with an inspirational work ethic, Trevelyan visited Ireland just once during his term in office at which time, October 1847, he remained in Dublin. Trevelyan apparently did not wish to have his judgment clouded by exposure to emotive distraction. It is equally clear that his studied disengagement from the consequences of his actions bordered on the irrational. Far from being a cloistered maverick who exploited cabinet dissension to experiment with ruinous economic policies, Trevelyan's efforts in Ireland won the fulsome praise of influential Whig colleagues. They ensured that he was awarded a knighthood in April 1848 in specific recognition of his Irish duties. Trevelyan's personal role in exacerbating the Great Famine cannot be divorced from general Whig attitudes and practices.

The notion that the spectre of Famine was detected sufficiently early in 1845 to enable preventative measures to be taken by the Tories does not exculpate the Whig Government from prime responsibility for the deadly results of its inaction in 1846. The trauma of 1845 was a harbinger of mass death which Russell, when in office, doggedly refused to heed. By early August 1846 Russell's cabinet, while divided on aspects of economic policy, had nonetheless agreed an inept relief strategy for Ireland. Early signs of acute problems had been established in July and it was in the full light of this realisation that Russell and Trevelyan scaled down the emergency provisions operated under

Peel. Most food depots were closed by August 1846 having been emptied of stocks which were deliberately run down owing to decisions taken in London. Only the most token level of additional supplies was subsequently amassed. It was acknowledged by the Whigs that the region to the west of the River Shannon would almost certainly require grain supplied by government in the event of the total failure of the potato crop. Even then, it was planned to withhold such food from sale until private local merchants had sold their stores.

Obsessive Whig adherence to free market principles ensured that their proxies were extremely slow to obtain any food earmarked for Ireland. In August to September 1846, a mere 7,600 tonnes of food, mostly maize, was imported from the Continent. This amount was insufficient to replenish the depots of Connacht and totally inadequate to build a meaningful national reserve. They had moved far too late for far too little. Time lapses certainly played a part in reducing the scale of the Whig response but only because the option of North American imports had been closed on *laissez-faire*-inspired ideological grounds without compensatory activity in British and Continental markets. Another solution was to buy part or all of the strong Irish oats harvest which in September 1846 had already provided the British economy with around 42,000 tonnes of produce. Routh of the Army Commissariat in Dublin complained to Trevelyan that non-acquisition and retention of this surplus in Ireland was 'a most serious evil'.[53] He knew that increased mortality was the real price of sending Irish grain to England. This was one of a litany of failures in mid-term planning and the state's negligence in procuring adequate supplies created a 'starvation gap' between the ruined potato harvest of August 1846 and the belated

importation of maize during the winter. No other power in the Western world mishandled its Famine crisis so badly.

Despite Whig posturing, 'Indian Corn' had been a politically astute move by the Tories. It was available at reasonable bulk prices owing to the Repeal of the Corn Laws and obtainable from overseas suppliers who did not displace British producers. Maize was grown in Britain and Ireland in the early 1840s, but, unlike wheat or oats, not in quantities sufficient to constitute a distinct internal market of consequence. Russell was clear on this key point in October 1846 when he reiterated that 'all that we have undertaken with respect to food … is to endeavour to create a provision trade, at fair mercantile prices, where no provision trade has hitherto existed'. This was quite a different objective to saving Irish subjects from starvation and indicative that counter-Famine initiatives had strategic ulterior motives from the start. For Russell, 'the infliction of Providence' had simply exposed Irish overdependence on the potato and its 'loss … will only aggravate the woes and sufferings of Ireland'. This was correct insofar as blight was a chance occurrence and that the severity of its impact was linked to long-term circumstances. Incredibly, Russell divined no Imperial responsibility for allowing such a state of affairs to come into being and was thus less disposed to redress state failures than should have been the case. By late 1846 Russell remained irritated by the inability of the bickering scientists to categorise the 'unknown miasma'. The uncertainties this posed in relation to root crop production reinforced his opinion that Ireland's agricultural economy 'must be greatly improved' by emulating the English.[54]

Incompetence and ideology were a deadly combination. Westminster rendered itself incapable of forestalling starvation within the United Kingdom. Blight was a natural

phenomenon, but failure to respond to its infestation was entirely a matter of human attitude and ability. Unlike their counterparts in Continental Europe, the British Government placed no restrictions on grain and food exports from Ireland and thereby jeopardised the lives of the many for the enrichment of the few. This was not deemed morally justified elsewhere. Even if withholding Irish produce at source proved unequal to fully resolving the task in hand, a deliberately rejected option, intervention of this kind would have alleviated pressure on imports, if not also inflation. The fortunes of Ireland's reasonably healthy food exporters were unlikely to implode if acceptable prices were negotiated and paid for in-country instead of on the far shores of England and Wales. The informed judgment of the Army Commissariat in Dublin was not discounted on the assumption that it was inaccurate but rather on the basis that it did not accord with the wider requirements of the planned new economy.

Official grain trade figures for 1846 reveal something of the potential for redirecting Irish produce towards relief. In return for some 62,955 tonnes of wheat imported from Britain and elsewhere, 84,399 tonnes of Irish wheat and flour was exported. Whereas a mere 3,726 tonnes of foreign oats arrived in the country, a virtual fleet exported 183,451 tonnes from Irish docks. Barley imports topped 7,295 tonnes in 1846 when 16,751 tonnes were conveyed overseas. By far the most important inflow of food was the 121,612 tonnes of maize. Even though the vast bulk of maize was landed for private sale, there is no doubt but that this accretion was significant in offsetting the general loss of Irish produce.[55] The two major beneficiaries were the Irish merchants who could sell on to those in possession of cash and the English economy which needed imported

food. Between November 1845 and January 1846 32,883 cattle, 32,576 sheep and 104,141 pigs were shipped to Britain from Ireland. Despite such strong exports, those who could pay for food in Ireland would survive unless unfortunate enough to be felled by disease. Statistical analyses of the United Kingdom grain trade in 1846-7 conceal the reality of its inevitable byproducts in Ireland; mass death, contagion and forced emigration. Anti-Irishness, 'moralism' and evangelical 'Providentialism' may have strengthened the resolve of the leading Whigs to persevere with their doctrinaire economics, but such prejudices reinforced rather than inspired their legislative responses.[56]

5. POPULAR RESISTANCE

A violent reaction to grain exports was virtually assured in a country with such strong traditions of agrarian insurgency. From the 1760s the Whiteboys and other oath-bound groups had used demonstrations of solidarity and tactics of intimidation to protest perceived threats to the rural poor. In the early decades of the 1800s tithe proctors and other perceived oppressors were periodically targeted for assassination. Similar manifestations of popular anger could not be discounted in the crisis of the mid-1840s. Fear of rebellion prompted the Mayor of Limerick, E.F.G. Ryan, to lead a deputation to Dublin on 23 March 1846 to urge the Relief Commission to commence public works before the city men took matters into their own hands.[57] In January 1846 it had proved necessary to read the Riot Act and open fire on a huge crowd resisting evictions in the Castleconnell area. Two constables were shot and wounded in a related incident in Annacotty.[58] General Edward Pine Coffin, Deputy Commissary of Limerick's 'Indian Corn' depot, concurred with Ryan's forecast in March. Limerick was then a major storage point for Munster produce bound for export and, in the event of trouble, the city had over fifty resident constables and a sizeable army garrison. No chances were taken in neighbouring Tipperary in April 1846 when grain being packed onto barges in Clonmel received a military escort. Fifty cavalry, eighty infantry and two cannon ensured that the food bound for export from Waterford passed safely to the staging town of Carrick-on-Suir. At least £100,000 worth of food was escorted from Ireland between July 1845 and February 1846.[59]

The realisation that a second year of Famine loomed created panic in many sectors during the autumn. The sense of 'alarm and apprehension' in Cork in early September 1846 led to public meetings in Fermoy, Mallow, Bantry, Middleton and other towns.[60] Cork Examiner reported on 16 September that workmen of the Fitzgerald family of Rocklodge, Cloyne, 'refused to allow him to send his corn to Cork [city], or to market, and stated that they would give him the price he demanded for it. To this step they said they were compelled by the loss of their potatoes, and the dearness of provisions'. Rumours then abounded of 'intended risings' but the calming advice of clergy and the pre-emptive dispatch of dragoons to the port of Youghal from Cork city were deemed constructive. Within a week serious unrest had broken out in Youghal, where the contentious grain and emigrants crowded the same docks. A 'concourse' of the 'labouring classes' moved onto the quay to demonstrate against the impending transferral of food to at least twelve merchantmen waiting offshore to carry it abroad. Having initially shown restraint, soldiers intervened non-violently when bread and flour merchants in the town were menaced. Local magistrate, J. Keily, discerned a dangerous escalation and sought additional military reinforcements to deter any further interference with commerce.[61]

The *Waterford Freeman*, in an account picked up by the *Cork Examiner* on 18 September, noted that 'impoverished labourers' had also become 'riotous' in Waterford when they realised the Presentment Sessions in Dungarvan was going to close without approving the 'immediate works' needed to inject cash into the regional economy. Light wounds to a constable and a soldier of the 27th Regiment were amongst the 'many injuries' sustained in keeping

public order and carrying out arrests in the port town. The conflagration was sparked by the coincidence of an unexpected hiatus in public works commencement with the concentration locally of a major consignment of food for overseas markets. Both issues posed a lethal threat to the rioters.[62] Dungarvan witnessed the first known fatal food riot of the Famine on 28 September 1846. Captain Sibthorp and the First Royal Dragoons were on hand to guard food stores assembled for export and stood by while the Riot Act was read to a restive crowd of onlookers. Having warned the protestors that they faced summary justice if they persisted, Sibthorp's dragoons dispersed the crowd on Old Chapel Road by attacking them head on. At least two men were shot dead by the troopers and several others were wounded. This ruthlessness followed incidents in Cloyne and Castlemartyr in preceding days where bakeries were looted by desperate labourers living in the surrounding countryside. In general, fewer incidents occurred than might have been expected under the circumstances.

While more restrained in Waterford than legally permitted, the authorities were determined to uphold the rule of law insofar as it pertained to the business of the grain trade. Henry Labouchere, Chief Secretary of Ireland in Dublin Castle, issued a proclamation on 2 October 1846 threatening to use 'every means' to prevent 'illegal proceedings' such as raids on merchants and making demands for higher wages on relief schemes.[63] This was largely bluff as the military and constabulary were disinclined to invoke the *carte blanche* of martial law. One Quinn was committed to Waterford Gaol for refusing to give evidence against a young Dungarvan rioter named Fleming. Quinn declared: 'Whatever would be the consequence he never would prosecute hungry people who offered no harm or violence

to person or property'. This stance did not save Fleming who succumbed to gunshot wounds to his knee in early November after a slow decline in the workhouse. By then, of the fifty-one suspected Waterford rioters called before the Quarter Sessions of Dungarvan, only 'ringleader' Patrick Power was imprisoned. The twelve-month sentence imposed on Power was deemed light as it was the prerogative of the court to order his transportation. Wisely, the county authorities adopted a calming policy of leniency. This may have been suggested by uncertainty as to whether jurors could be found who were willing to back the severe punishments available under the Riot Act.[64]

The frustration of the Irish protesters struck a chord with some English commentators, including those vehemently opposed to Repeal of the Union. A writer in the *Pictorial Times* of 10 October 1846 sympathised with those living within sight of food they could not afford. He stated: 'Property laws supersede those of Nature. Grain is of more value than blood. And if they attempt to take of the fatness of the land that belongs to their lords, death by musketry is a cheap government measure to provide for the wants of a starving and incensed people. This must not be'. In the event, gunfire and the gallows claimed an infinitesimal fraction of those who died in the fields, cottages and workhouses in 1846-7.

Crisis, October / November 1846

As expected, the onset of winter brought widespread hardship and numerous premature deaths. Irish press reports of the early fatalities were often highly detailed and self-consciously legalistic in tone. This reflected, to a large degree, the utilisation of information obtained from the

proceedings of coroners' courts. However, there was frequently an editorial line which suggested an interest in amassing evidence of an unfolding tragedy. The purpose was not simply to memorialise those who had died, or to inform the general public of the scale of the disaster, but to marshal irrefutable data which could not be dismissed in Westminster. In the absence of a national government, the House of Commons was the only forum with the capacity to intervene with decisive effect. The minutiae of accounts in the regional Irish media, therefore, was a persuasive device to elicit a level of relief which the country's MPs, Dublin Castle and the Viceroy had collectively failed to deliver.

The death from starvation of Daniel Hayes of Lorrha, Tipperary, was related by the Munster press in late October 1846. A coroner found on 24 October that Hayes had lived for several days on vegetable scraps and collapsed and died when searching for more substantial food.[65] Starvation-related deaths were then claiming increasing numbers from the south coast and north west, as noted in the *Kerry Examiner* and *Mayo Constitution*. Coroners' reports in Kerry for John Botend of Dingle and John Browne of Kilquane found that the men had died in mid-November 1846 from a combination of hunger, exhaustion and exposure. Botend expired while labouring on public works and Browne when making his way home to Dingle from Tralee workhouse. In Mayo, one Williams of Foxford died on his way to the Swinford workhouse whereas Thomas Hopkins of Crossmolina succumbed at home in front of his wife and five children. For six weeks the Hopkins family had eaten 'a scanty morsel on some days, and on others were obliged to remain without it'.[66] Fasting was evidently common. By late December the scale of death in Mayo was such that

Above: *The Irish Famine* by George Frederic Watts, 1850, shows a distressed Irish family.

Left: Searching the fields for food.

The Humble Memorial of the undernam
the Tenantry of Thomas Conry Esq &c

Gentlemen

We the undernamed having each of
us tickets signed by your Honourable Chairman
and two other Gentlemen of Your Committe
beg leave most humbly and respectfully to state
That we are this fortnight without employment
When we go to Mr Barton he would tell us apply
to Mr Warnock, and when we go to Mr Warnock he
sends us back to Mr Barton — In Speaking to Mr
Barton today he says he must break 100 Men more
out of the Work, and thus we have no hope of relief
from him — And what must we do — Our families
really and truly suffering in our present and we
cannot much longer withstand their cries for food
We have no food for them Our potatoes are rotten
and we have no grain — And Gentlemen — You know but
very little of the State of the suffering poor — If Mr Barton
knew our state he should not adopt the policy of breaking
100 Men More to protract the Work instead of giving
us employment But Gentlemen We must cry out
against the policy of protracting the Work for the few, while
we are suffering from famine and distress and the
Want of employment — Are we to Resort to outrage — We
have peaceably and quietly conducted ourselves and
patiently submitted to the Will of Divine Providence
and cannot restrain from expressing to your our
feelings, and our wrongs, Gentlemen We fear
that the peace of the Country will be much disturbed
if relief be not immediately, more extensively
afforded to the suffering peasantry, We are not
for joining in any thing illegal or contrary to
the laws of God or the land unless pressed to
by HUNGER, we are willing to work, and hope Gentn
you will take part in remedying our present
Calamity by giving us employment or by getting

Facing page: The first page of a desperate petition from the tenants of Cloonahee, Elphin, County Roscommon; they had been turned away from the relief works. It reads: 'Our families are really and truly suffering ... We cannot much longer withstand their cries for food ... Our potatoes are rotten and we have no grain ...'

This page, above: A scene of destitution as the potato harvest fails.

[illegible]	6	A[illegible]	
[illegible]	6	John Lyons	3
onnell Hopkins	6	Widow Feeney	5
hn Hopkins	4	Widow Cline	4
hn Murry	1	Michael Goggins	5
dow Cox	6	Widow Lyons	7
dow Cox	4	Patt Wallace	6
on Greene, sen.	6	Patt Smyth	6
ddow Greene	4	Widow Feeney	1
mes Greene, jun.	6	Patt Feeney	7
ames Greene	3	John Feeney	4
ke Greene	3	James Lyons	5
rtin Greene	4	Luke Lyons	6
ke Feeney	4	Michael Cawneen	3
minick Feeney	1	John Greene	6

Total (including seven widows), 134 souls.

LOWER CULLAGH.

rtin Wallace	5	Peter Cox	3
tt Wallace	9	Widow Mannion	5
chael Wallace	9	James M'Neal	7
mes Wallace	7	Michael Mullooly	6
mes Wallace	7	Michael Cox	5
en M'Neal	6	Widow Mullooly	4
dow Lyons	5	James Cunningham	6
mes Gavan	6	Martin Cox	5
tt Clyne	6	John M'Neal	5
chael Doyle	4	Daniel Mullooly	4
niel Connor	3	Michael Kain	7

Total (including three widows), 124 souls.

GURTFUSE.

hn Murphy	11	Thomas M'Cormick	6
mes Dooly	4	Bryan Doyle	6
t Murphy	4	Pat M'Guire	4
ke Murray	7	James M'Guire	10
dow Murray	11	John Madden	5
dow Brennan	4	James Murphy	2
mes Long	4	James Madden	4
chael Murphy	7	Michael Murphy	4
chael Coogan	4	Thady Kennedy	5
ward Holmes	5	Pat Cassidy	4
omas Hanly	3	William Holmes	5
lliam M'Neal	8	Peter Lyons	7
t M'Neal	7	Pat Kilkenny	4
chael M'Neal	11	Cannon M'Guire	6
t Donohoe	5	Daniel M'Guire	4
omas Donohoe	3	Widow M'Guire	6
ke Farrell	8		

Total (including three widows) 145 souls.

MAHON'S YARD.

dow Donohoe	5	John Hedian	5
ggy Rogers	3	Michael Hedian	4
chael Kain	7	Widow Healy	5
mes Hedean	6	John Connor	3
hn Cox	7	Martin Connor	2
omas Moran	6	John Connor	4
nifred Rowan	1	Andrew Connor	3
dow Moran	4	Thomas Quinn	7
dow Kean	2	Nancy Kelly	1
t Horse	6	Thady Fihily	5
ter Murray	6	Martin M'Guinness	6
omas Cox	7	Daniel Hogan	5
hn Fihily	4	Daniel Beirne	5
hn Bohan	6	John Beirne	5
chael Fihily	7	Pat Cox	1
t Cox	4	Frank Bohannon	5
idget Oates	3	Bernard Doyle	6
ward Hogan	5	William Connor	4
ers Williams	3	Pat Murray	2
rby Carlos	7	James Hopkins	5
dow Mullen	9	Pat Shanly	5
t Murray	7	Martin Fox	5
ke Murray	3	Bryan Sharvan	6
chael Cox	6	James Sharvan	9
dow Hedian	7	James Sharvan	4
chael Hedian	7	Anne M'Guire	6
dow Kelly	4	Bryan Kelly	6
nard Ford	8	Michael M'Dermott	7
dow Conolly	1	James Killion	5
rtin Feeny	4	John Long	6
chael Feeny	4	Michael M'Evoy	3
ank Flanagan	6	Pat Foard	8
rrell Murray	1	Thomas Foard	3
chael Forde	10	John Keelty	6
mes Kelly	7	John Moran	6
hn Kelly	6	Michael Killion	6
dow Gill	2	Anne Kelly	1

Total (including six widows) 3?6 souls.

CURDRUMMIN.

gh Murry	6	John Murry	5
ke Murry	6	Peter Murry	3
omas Hagan	6	Michael Clabby	6
dow Murry	5	Patt M'Garry	3
chael Murry	8	James Kelly	4
chael Cox	9	Thomas Cox	5
ke Murry	5	Bridget Hagan	1

Total, 7? souls.

Phelim Hanly	8	Carberry Duff	
Edward Hanly	6	Thomas Egan	
John Egan	6	Michael Fallon	
Thomas Callery	4	Patt Hogan	
Thomas Egan	4	Thomas Dillon	
James Duffey	5	Widow Cavern	
Patt Fallon	4	Hugh Kelly	
Gilbert Beirne	3	Widow Shaug	
John Fallon	6	Patt Bolan	
William Fihily	5	Michael Teer	
James Flood	11	Patt Dowd	
Owen Fallon	4	Michael Coug	
Thomas Fallon	6	Patt Feeney	
Widow Duffy	3	Widow Gann	
Michael Beirne	7	Widow Beirne	

Total (including six widows), 135

LUGBOY.

James Gilloran	3	Andrew Con	
John Moran	6	Michael Duf	
Patt Gannon	6	Michael Duf	
Edward Keogh	3	Widow M'D	
Patt Crosby	5	John Tracey	
Patt Tracey	3	Edward Han	
Thady Mongan	4	Widow Bret	
Thady Duffy	4	Edward Duf	
James Duffy	6	Edward Duf	
John M'Giff	3		

Total (including two widows), [illegible]

TULLYCARTRON.

Michael M'Hugh	6	Bryan Conc	
Martin M'Hugh	6		

Total, 14 souls.

CLOONEY BRENNAN.

Ned Marks	2	Thomas Ma	
Patt M'Loughlin	5	John Kelly	
James Feeney	6		

Total, 2? souls.

CLOONRAINE.

John Powell	4	James Farre	
James Powell	6	Michael Far	
Michael Brennan	6	Mary Anne	
Hugh Towey	6	Michael Flyn	
Thomas Kaveney	3	Martin Bren	
Sally M'Donnell	1	Thomas Bre	
Margaret M'Donnell	1	Michael Far	
Widow Ward	4	Widow Beir	
Mary Doherty	5	Margaret Br	
John Nugent	7	Mary Powell	
Widow Scally	4	Mary Barry	
Ellen Donoher	4	Kitty Walla	
Peter Dempsey	6		

Total (including three widows), 9

TOOREEN.

Patt Moraghan	3	James Fallon	
Widow M'Dermott	5	Patt Fallon	
Widow Quinne	3	Michael Bar	
Widow M'Namara	4	Widow Gav	
Mathias Croghan	2	Michael Sau	
John Maxwell	3	Roger Quinn	
Patt Hanly	8	Luke Fallon	
Richard Saunders	5	James Saund	

Total (including four widows), [illegible]

KILMACNANENY.

Pat Corcoran	8	Stephen Lar	
Widow Harry Noon	7	Bryan Horal	
John Fallon	6	James Grealy	
John Monaghan	5	Pat Mahon	
Peter Monaghan	7	Pat Mahon,	
William Campbell	4	Thomas Cor	
John Corcoran	4	Michael Cam	
Wm Campbell, sen	1	Widow No	
Widow Campbell	6	Michael Kea	
Widow Kelly	7	William	
Thomas Brennan	3	Michael Gav	
Edward Kelly	6	Thomas Gill	
Widow James Noone	1	Michael Gill	
Pat M'Neal	6	Widow Flan	
Thomas Connellan	6	Thady Murr	
Pat Campbell	3	John Duffy	
Pat Kelly	7	Bryan Dono	
Bryan Lennon	5	Bryan Conn	
Bridget Kelly	3	Widow Bren	
William Corcoran	4	Loughlin K	
Widow Padean	4	Pat Mahon	
Michael M'Guire	4		

Total (including 8 widows), 112

CURHOWNAGH.

Peter Clements	7	James Mull	
John Coleman	5	James Kelly	
Michael Lennon	7	Thomas Re	
Thomas Deenase	1	James Sheri	
Dolly Connolly	2	Owen Kelly	
Roger Quinn	5	Michael Da	
James Quinn	6	Lachey Don	

Total, 18 souls.

AUGHADINE.

John Reynolds	6	John Duffy	

Facing page: Part of a list from the *Freeman's Journal* 29 April 1848, listing 3,006 persons evicted by the Mahon family from their lands, Strokestown Estate, County Roscommon.

This page, above: Tenants plead with a bailiff on horseback as they are evicted from their home.

This page below: the workhouse at Lismore, County Waterford.

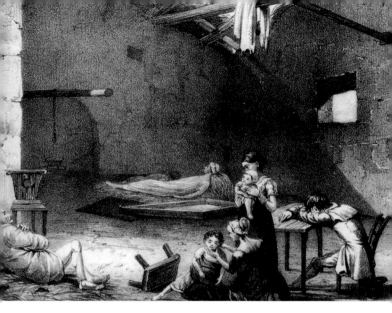

THE ENGLISH LABOURER'S BURDEN;

Or, THE IRISH OLD MAN OF THE MOUNTAIN.

[See *Sinbad the Sailor.*]

Above: The interior of a miserable cabin, show-ing sick and dying family members.

Left: Political cartoon, showing the industrious English labourer carrying the Irishman on his shoulders; the Irishman is carrying a sack of money, presumably aid received from England.

Above: Food riots in Dungarvan, County Waterford.
Below: Irish emigrants waiting at the Liverpool docks for a ship to America.

Above: Abandoned house in a 'Famine village', Achill, County Mayo.
Below: Rowan Gillespie's 'Famine' sculpture, Custom House Quay, Dublin.

biographical details often had to be omitted by journalists due to spatial considerations. One aggravated correspondent specified that the coroner's courts had recently verified forty-seven fatalities in the county where 'political economy is doing its bloody work'.[67]

It was reported on 4 December 1846 that William J. Maher presided at an inquest at Corbetstown, Kilkenny, into the deaths of four people in a dyke at Webbsborough. The court heard that the woman and three children aged nine and younger received basic charity from a local family, but that the mother had been subsequently observed 'in an unconscious state, probably from mental anxiety and hunger'. They were not sighted again until their muddied, ragged and frozen bodies were pulled from the dyke. Postmortem results showed that the woman had not eaten for over twenty hours prior to drowning and the children were 'in a state of hunger bordering on starvation'. Something of the horror of the scenario was revealed when Dr Gwydir of Freshford testified that rats had gnawed the bodies of two of the children. The verdict of the coroner's jury implied a finding of infanticide and suicide whilst claiming lack of 'evidence' to avoid a stigmatic explicit assertion to this effect.[68]

The unfortunate Kilkenny family would not have been assured of salvation inside a workhouse. James Crosfield visited several Roscommon workhouses in December 1846 and found evidence of worsening conditions arising from their inappropriate utilisation in Famine-relief mode. Crosfield explained: 'At the Castlerea workhouse a shocking state of things existed, the poor inmates lying upon straw and their dormitories being in such a state of dirt that we were unable to venture into them. In this workhouse there are at present 1,080 paupers, but the last 434 were admitted

in so hurried a manner that there is neither bedding nor clothes for them; it is probable that there will be frightful mortality amongst the inmates. In the children's room was collected a miserable crowd of wretched objects, the charm of infancy having entirely disappeared and in its place were to be seen wan and haggard faces'.[69]

Captain Edward Wynne, District Inspector for West Clare of the Poor Law Commission, was deeply disturbed by his experiences that month. Having found no bread for sale at any price in Ennis, Wynne was equally unsettled by the realisation that no domestic animals could be seen in the surrounding countryside. He knew that a police guard was necessary to prevent the over-full workhouse from being besieged and that the people he saw in the parishes had nowhere to go. With this in mind he was 'unmanned by the extent of the suffering' he witnessed. Wynne reported to the Board of Works that he had observed 'women and little children, crowds of whom were to be seen scattered over the turnip fields, like a flock of famished crows, devouring the raw turnips, mothers half naked, shivering in the snow and sleet, uttering exclamations of despair whilst their children were screaming with hunger … the Public Works must fail in keeping the population alive'.[70]

Death in Skibbereen

The Fenian icon Jeremiah O'Donovan Rossa was sixteen in 1847 when the tide of Famine engulfed the Roscarberry district of Cork. The family, at first, fared better than others and generously opened their doors to eight less fortunate refugees from hunger and eviction. The path from economic vulnerability to displacement and starvation was all too short. Within days of arrival the newcomers secretly killed

and ate their donkey, a mystery quietly debated by their concerned hosts. Within a few months of offering shelter to the strangers O'Donovan Rossa's father starved to death.[71]

Skibbereen, Cork, attained international notoriety for its particularly high concentration of mortality. British and North American readers were appalled by stories of wretchedness and death. The town attracted the attention of the *Cork Examiner* on 25 November 1846 when the coroner failed to turn up for an inquest into the deaths of three men from starvation. Pressure of work was cited as the main reason. However, it was also rumoured that officials of the Board of Works were 'averse' to a formal examination of 'the cause of this dreadful mortality' in the district lest it expose their negligence. In early January 1847, 700 local men approved for employment by the Relief Committee were unable to secure labour and life-saving pay on the public works. There were simply not enough places on the schemes. Instead, the rebuffed heads of families were obliged to join the hopeless search for private charity in a place where 'in every house ... there is death'.[72] John Driscoll, Poor Rate Collector in the parish of Schull, called to the Regans of Rossbrin to find three 'lifeless corpses'. Moving on to nearby Drishane, Driscoll was shaken when he found Mrs Neill and three of her children dead. They lay near the man of the house who appeared deceased but was actually 'lying sick'.[73] At Bantry, where the French military had failed to land in aid of the United Irishmen in December 1796, the coroners were overwhelmed by the multiple 'Holocausts offered at the shrine of political economy' and simply could not keep pace with the death toll from starvation. In Kilmoe parish an anonymous victim was partially eaten by dogs before his body was found.[74]

The capital was far less afflicted but by no means immune. In early January 1847 it was reported:

'Notwithstanding the unprecedented arrivals of grain into the port of Dublin, prices still continue to advance. At the Corn Exchange today considerable excitement prevailed and wheat, according to official market note, went up 1s. 6d ... Before 8 o'clock this morning a mob consisting of between 40 and 50 persons, many of them boys, commenced an attack upon the baker's shops in the neighbourhood of Summer Hill, Britain Street and Abbey Street. Owing to their early hour and the unexpectedness of the outbreak, they were enabled to carry on their depredations without let or hindrance. The rioters had the appearance of country people, and came from the northern outlets of the city. When they had reached Abbey Street two policemen interfered, and endeavoured to disperse the crowd, but without any effect, several men exclaiming that they had been without food for twenty-four hours, and that bread they should have. They had then marched 'in close order' towards Mary's Street, where there are great numbers of provision and cookshops'.[75]

Anxious to ascertain the veracity of these sensational news stories, Irishmen Lord Dufferin and George Frederick Boyle made a week-long visit to Ireland from Oxford in late February 1847. They jointly published a pamphlet on their findings as *Narrative of a journey from Oxford to Skibbereen during the year of the Irish Famine*. They began their tour in Dublin, where food riots had taken place the previous month, and noted the efficient workings of soup kitchens in Athy, Kildare.[76] Only 'some deaths' had occurred at that stage in Kildare, insufficient to register major concern. They witnessed the steady deterioration of conditions as they neared West Cork where they claimed were directed

to see the full onslaught of Famine. The men had not been misled and the first sight encountered in their approach to Skibbereen was 'nine or ten deal coffins'. A representative of the village Relief Committee explained how its formerly industrious inhabitants had been reduced by hunger and typhus to sell their furniture, possession, nets and boats to buy food. An entire community had plummeted from self-sufficiency to calamity with startling speed.

It was claimed that sixty-five people per week died in the workhouse where 1,449 were then 'crammed' into a space designed for 800. As its doors were closed to further admissions, thirty-five to forty persons died elsewhere every day in the district with a pre-Famine population of 20,000. Debilitation and disease complicated the management of mortality on this scale. Removing corpses proved difficult owing to the amount of hazardous and demanding labour involved in collecting, transporting and burying bodies. Religious observances, let alone traditional rites of keening and wakes, were then generally eschewed. Bodies from the workhouse and hovels were interred in shallow unmarked graves in mere shrouds. This offered no real protection against disinterment by animals and the resultant pestilence and putrefaction posed an additional risk to public health.

Departing Skibbereen was described by Dufferin and Boyle in terms befitting a gothic horror novel, as the authors may well have intended in order to best convey their chilling message. A large crowd of desperate women literally besieged the pair seeking a small supply of loaves they had bought with the intention of distributing en route to Dublin. Fearing, in all probability, the ill-effects of direct contact with a 'fighting', 'screaming' and 'swaying ... human mass', the loaves were unceremoniously tossed to

the crowd from the vantage of a window. This distraction enabled the men to hurry out of the house in safety. When mounted, the travellers passed with 'some difficulty' through the people; 'horses careering about in all directions, and the strongest of the multitude running by our side'. Thus extricated from a vividly-related scene of terror, they queried: 'what legislation and what influences' could make West Cork 'industrious and independent'. Coming from members of the Establishment, the grisly account provided a vindication of sorts for Britons who had contributed to the many private Famine charities. Examples of positive intervention recorded by Dufferin and Boyle were counter-pointed with others of landlord neglect and its harrowing consequences. Oxford publisher John Henry Parker printed three editions before the end of 1847 and donated the proceeds to the relief effort in Skibbereen.[77]

By no means all inhabitants of the United Kingdom viewed events in compassionate terms. The quasi-religious cult of 'providence' excited all manner of evangelical enthusiasts in Famine-stricken Ireland. Adherents believed that the Famine was God's punishment for the immoral and irreligious conduct of its victims. Rev. Thomas Hanley preached a particularly vitriolic sermon on this theme in Mullabrack, Armagh, on 24 March 1847 which queried why 'JEVOHAH' had 'manifested his anger by laying bare his arm'. Hanley's outrageous explanation of Famine would have angered a considerable proportion of Armagh natives by ascribing their misfortune to such factors as 'inactivity', 'infidelity', 'filthy conversation', 'Sabbath-breaking', 'Drunkenness', 'Robbery' and 'Murder'. This ludicrous litany, the product of a disordered and bigoted mind, held out no prospect of salvation, deliverance or justified survival. With final insult, Hanley approved 'hell's torment' for those

'who, unprovoked, and with cool, calculating premeditation, waylays his fellow-man, and sends the innocent victim to an unmerited and untimely grave'. The extremity of Hanley's delusions were such that he evidently merited the silent deaths of hundreds of thousands of men, women and children over the actions of a few dozen partisans who sought to resist by means of well publicised acts of violence.[78]

Sermons of this nature had nothing to offer the unfortunate victims of 'Famine Fever' in Newry, Enniskillen, Downpatrick and Belfast, or those dying from starvation in March 1847 in Galway and Queen's County (Laois). Fifty to sixty persons died every week in Belfast workhouse and approximately fifty a week in Lurgan, Armagh. Linen wages in Lurgan and Portadown were insufficient to permit total independence of the potato crop and many Presbyterian workers died in consequence. As in Skibbereen, the high numbers and diseased state of the dead resulted in the abandonment of Christian norms in Shankill, Friar's Bush and Clifton Street cemeteries, Belfast. Emaciated and disease-ridden corpses were hastily dumped into grave pits, which contained hundreds and, in the case of Clifton Street, thousands of people. Famine dead filled the old graveyards and, when the population surged once more in its aftermath, necessitated the opening of Belfast City Cemetery, Ballymurphy.[79]

6. THE END OF PUBLIC WORKS

The blight of 1846 assailed the social fabric of rural Ireland by permanently shattering the economy of conacre farming. Potatoes were neither obtainable as a food source, nor as a means of paying rent. The small holders, therefore, needed cash as never before to purchase food and meet their rental obligations. Yet small landlords could not afford to pay workers owing to the overall un-productivity of the marginal property occupied by their tenants and the high concentration of labourers in need of money. Flight of workers to public works and then into workhouses further undermined the tenure of interdependent low income classes. Rent arrears and rate demands accumulated.

Worse, by 1847, a combination of under-planting and mounting scarcity of healthy seed potatoes made for chronic conditions of suffering and death. Public works were no longer either cost-effective or efficient in providing the Irish poor with the means to obtain food with cash. Far more people sought employment than could be paid or properly administered. In late January 1847 the Whigs were obliged to concede that the range of minor modifications imposed by Trevelyan was inadequate and that another form of relief was required. Essentially, the Poor Law network would be used for a new type of 'indoor relief', but not until the autumn when the crop situation and inclement weather would play major roles in shaping definitive responses. In the interim, food would be distributed by soup kitchens to stave off mass mortality.[80]

The closing of public works schemes had a serious short-term impact as it deprived hundreds of thousands of the most able-bodied Famine survivors of the means to

earn a subsistence wage. Whatever cash such men had managed to save was inflated beyond usefulness by the continued scarcity of affordable food. It remained extremely difficult for those in reasonable health to turn their labour into financial independence. Moreover, the chance glut of cheap American corn in Europe ensured that the small farmers who had managed to cultivate modest quantities of grain for harvest in 1847 required this precious surplus to cover their rent. It could not be either consumed or sold for real profit as grain prices were depressed by American imports. More grain than ever was required for paying rent and persons who failed to meet their commitments to landlords were subject to immediate eviction. London persisted in encouraging a hard line with defaulters and suspected malingerers as such inflexibility underpinned laissez faire. Yet, incontrovertible proof of severe hardship came in the autumn of 1847 when those discharged from the public works were incapable of buying the partially improved potato crop. The deaths of thousands answered the queries of those in London who doubted the gravity of their predicament.

Soup kitchens

Many construction projects had discharged their workers before the Destitute Persons (Ireland) Act created alternate modes of food supply in January 1847. Further variants of the 'Soup Kitchen Act' and 'Burgoyne's Act' followed in February 1847 which nominally reaffirmed the role of the workhouse and the Irish Poor Law Commission in large-scale relief operations. More generally, the Act restated the principle of Irish fiscal responsibility for what continued to be viewed as an Irish problem. Westminster

remained unconvinced that it had a decisive role to play in Famine avoidance. However, the pioneering charitable enterprises of the Society of Friends (Quakers) had shown the great potential of soup kitchens in Cork in November 1846. Quakers also organised charitable relief in Clonmel, Tipperary, where they convened meeting on 2 November of 'all sects and classes' to establish a soup depot.[81] Private charity of this kind was crucial to spanning a dangerous period intervening the cessation of public works and commencement of official soup kitchens. A model kitchen was opened outside the Royal Barracks, Dublin, on 5 April 1847 by the French celebrity philanthropist and cook Alexis Soyer and it proved an ingenious and popular success. The Whigs pursued the chance to replace the controversial and expensive works with a relief measure that compromised the strict economic tenets of *laissez-faire*. This was palliated by the fact that soup kitchens were much cheaper and more easily managed than public works.[82]

By June 1847 around 95 per cent of those previously employed on public relief schemes had been discharged and effectively obliged to receive food rations directly from the new kitchens. This would not have presented a major problem if the Government's co-ordination of the discharges had kept pace with the establishment of the food distribution network. Instead, around one million people obtained rations from soup kitchens in May 1847 when a further 2.3 million labourers and dependents went without subvention. This revealed a lack of forward planning. While this imbalance had improved dramatically by July, it has been estimated that 15 per cent of those entitled to assistance in 1847 received none. Even this masked the real depth of the problem as the figures excluded the considerable numbers of deserving persons who had been denied

work on public schemes in the first place. The number of those who perished during the transition has never been established but it must have been high given that Skibbereen, a byword for Famine privation in the British media, did not receive its soup kitchen until June 1847. Ironically, this outlet transpired to be the last of its kind as Trevelyan signalled in July that the kitchens would close by October. This deadline, in every sense of the word, was later brought forward.

The government was confident, for no apparent reason, that the potato crop due in the autumn of 1847 would have made a strong recovery. The announcement of kitchen closures was palliated by another to the effect that the debts they had accrued would be cancelled. Outstanding debts of the public relief schemes would also be forgiven. While retrospectively assuming the financial burden of temporary outdoor relief undoubtedly struck proponents of liberal economics as generous, it did very little to improve conditions. The Government, however, had greatly enhanced its own financial position in that around £2.25 million had been channelled to the soup kitchens with approximately half funded by Irish Poor Law rates. Yet only £1.7 million, including costs incurred by fever hospital and salaries, had been spent by September 1847 when relief shuddered to a sudden halt. This figure contrasted with operating costs incurred by the public relief schemes of approximately £5.5 million of which less than half a million had been financed by Irish rates. The kitchens, therefore, were not only far more economic and humane than the public works, but moved the imperfect Irish relief model closer to the Whig ideal of minimal state interference in the market economy. The Poor Law Extension Act would enshrine further important precepts.

Unfortunately, a number of unanticipated factors combined to ensure that 1847 was the worst single year of the Famine rather than the one in which the corner of the nightmare was turned. Westminster's Irish policies, increasingly reactive, self-serving and ineffective, remained utterly divorced from the moral and practical responsibilities of national government. Once again, domestic financial and ideological problems in Britain dictated unworkable scenarios in Ireland.

Assisted passage and the 'coffin ships'

Evicted tenants and those in dire straits had very few options in 1847. Emigration was possible for those with some cash to spare and the residual stamina to reach the ports: Britain and North America were all deluged with wretched Irish immigrants. 50,000 arrived in Liverpool in March 1847, not much less than the normal annual outflow of Irishmen to North America from all ports. Internal migration was also considerable with Dublin, Limerick, Belfast and Cork receiving tens of thousands of starving migrants from the countryside.

Those who ventured across the Atlantic from Irish and British ports risked the hazards of travel in the so called 'coffin ships'. Such vessels were predominately a phenomenon of 1847 when urgency was great and official vigilance low. Amendments to the American Passenger Acts in March 1847 temporarily reduced the historic attractiveness of the country as a first destination. Even so, tens of thousands still ventured the familiar migrant paths to New York, Baltimore and Boston. New regulations taxed ship owners with headage charges and demanded standards of accommodation that reduced the profits of carrying high

numbers. The net effect was to increase the cost of travel to the United States to approximately £5 per person, whereas people conveyed in British ships to Canada could cross the Atlantic for less than £3 15 shillings.[83] As price was a considerable factor for both emigrants and captains, there was a major increase in the number of Irish refugees opting for Canadian ports in 1847. All too often the migrants heading for Quebec and Montreal were conveyed on timber vessels returning from European voyages rather than more suitable general cargo ships. Persons bound for the United States at the same time were more likely to be carried in ships which had landed cotton and tobacco.[84]

Masters seeking Irish passengers frequently published advertisements in the regional press such as the Wexford Independent. These often exaggerated their tonnage in order to evade Passenger Act laws that restricted persons embarked to three persons per five registered tonnes. Given the near limitless demand in Ireland for places, such ships almost invariably exceeded the legal capacity with dire health consequences. The huge surge in sea traffic produced maritime tragedies of a more conventional nature. In early May 1847 the *Exmouth* foundered on the coast of Islay (Scotland) causing the death of over 240 people going from Derry to Quebec. Other vessels struck ice in Canadian waters when risk-taking captains ventured to sea outside the optimum season for crossing the Atlantic.

One of the most important and successful series of migrations commenced in March 1847 from the 80,000 acre Coolattin estate in south Wicklow. It was owned by Charles Fitzwilliam (5th Earl Fitzwilliam) who as Lord Milton in the early 1830s, was a prominent supporter of the Whig Reform Bill. William Thomas Spencer Fitzwilliam, the earl's eldest son and MP for Wicklow in 1847, left the day to day running

of Coolattin to Robert Challoner senior. With the backing of
its owners, Challoner had taken a stand against subdivision on the estate. In early February 1847 tenants were
offered free passage to Canada and additional financial
inducements for those who required aid. Many could have
been simply and legally evicted for non-payment of rent.
Over three hundred families, totaling 2,000 persons, volun-
teered and complied with a requirement that their homes
be destroyed upon departure. Those who demolished their
own cabins were paid for the dispiriting task. Their holdings were then amalgamated into larger farming units. The
first batch of 317 emigrants left from New Ross, Wexford,
on the *Dunbrody* and were accompanied by an employee
of the estate who ensured that contract terms were met
during the passage. The *Dunbrody* reached Canada on 22
May 1847 having lost only five passengers en route. Six
more were landed in a feverish state but survived. By 1856,
6,000 of Fitzwilliam's tenants had crossed to New Bruns-
wick and Quebec at a cost of approximately £24,000.[85]
Investment, planning and oversight safeguarded the
Coolattin emigrants but this was far from typical.

The *Dunbrody*'s first voyage with Wicklow families
coincided with the seasonal opening of the ice prone St.
Lawrence River for navigation in late April/ early May.
Canada-bound immigrants were required to call to the
quarantine centre on Grosse Ille, thirty miles downriver
from Quebec. The first to do so on 14 May 1847 was the
Syria which had taken forty-six days to arrive from Liverpool. While only nine of its 254 Irish passengers had died
on board, at least half the remainder was infected with
typhus. The island's small hospital facility was quickly deluged when eight more shiploads of Famine refugees who
arrived between 19 and 21 May. Typhus and dysentery

were then widespread and forty of the *Syria* migrants died within a week of arrival. In the midst of this chaos, fifteen more vessels, including the *Dunbrody*, moored of Grosse Ille on 22 May with over 3,600 additional refugees for processing. In four days there were a total of thirty vessels and 10,000 passengers awaiting permission to disembark. A further thirty-six ships with another 13,000 people were present by 28 May. The swamped authorities on Grosse Ille struggled to fulfill their duties as more than fifty a day died awaiting disembarkation. By the end of the immigration season in early November 1847, around 78,700 Irish had passed through the station. It has been estimated that 5,424 were buried on Grosse Ille and 8,150 in the grounds of the Quebec and Ontario hospitals which treated fever victims. A further 4,100 were believed to have died at sea.[86] In all, around 50,000 Irish immigrants perished on the way to North America or shortly after arrival in 1847.[87]

Few first-hand accounts have survived of those who fled across the Atlantic. One extant journal was written by Gerald Keegan, who left Dublin for Canada shortly after marrying Aileen. The Keegans hailed from Kildare and Limerick and departed their native country with a small party of their relatives on 10 April 1847. One of Keegan's in-laws succumbed to 'a bad cold' on 29 April which had damaged her health while waiting to sail on the quays. His journal noted the following day:

The fever spreads and to the other horrors of the steerage is added cries of those in delirium. While coming from the galley the afternoon, with a pan of stirabout (i.e. porridge) for some sick children, a man suddenly sprang upwards from the hatchway, rushed to the bulwark, his white hair streaming in the wind, and without a moment's hesitation,

leaped into the seething waters … His daughter soon came hurrying up the ladder to look for him … Aileen led her away; dumb from the sudden stroke yet without a tear.

May 4, No death today. May 6, There were three deaths today. If it please God, may this agony soon end. May 9, Uncle's oldest son died of a fever … the body along with two more we dropped overboard when the sailors were at dinner … May 10, This was a sad day, five having died. May 11, A child died today, a sweet girl toddler that Aileen was fond of. Many of the sick are sinking tonight, not one of whom but might have lived with proper sustenance. May 12, Four deaths and the number of sick greatly increased'.[88]

Aileen Keegan died shortly after arriving at Grosse Ille, soon followed by her husband, who had assisted Father Moylan of Montreal in caring for the quarantined sick. His journal was obtained by a male relative on his mother's side who lived in Quebec. Poignantly, Keegan had written: 'May God have pity on me and on my poor people. Oh, that Aileen were here, that I felt her hand on my racked forehead'.[89]

Despite the extra charges involved, around 55 per cent of Irish emigrants went to the United States in 1847. As with those heading for Canada, the close confinement of fever stricken and malnourished persons was a recipe for disaster. Many had been embarked when unfit to travel and were neither treated nor separated from the healthy once at sea. The gruelling journey could take as long as six weeks, during which overcrowding, contagion and unsanitary conditions exacted a human toll. Savannah (Georgia), Charleston (South Carolina), Philadelphia (Pennsylvania), New Orleans (Louisiana) and the long familiar port cities of

the East Coast received hundreds of thousands of destitute Irish immigrants. After the horrendous experience of 1847 and the scandals it sparked in Britain, Canada and the United States, death rates on the ships reverted to normal ranges in 1848. Between 1845 and 1851, approximately 1.2 million Irish people migrated to North America where they were followed by a further 900,000 by 1855. Hundreds of thousands more settled in Britain where there were at least 727,326 Irish born residents in 1851 of whom 207,000 lived in Scotland. Imperial colonies, particularly Australia and New Zealand, also attracted large numbers despite the vastly increased costs of travel.[90]

Poor Laws and workhouses

Thousands of Famine victims availed of the workhouse, the sole official retreat available to the destitute under the Irish Poor Law. The Commission of Inquiry into the Famine noted as early as January 1846 that the 'poor houses will, without doubt, be found a most important means of relief … against a calamity more widely extended, and more serious in its nature, than any that has affected the Irish poor since the year 1817'. Severe problems, however, were encountered from the outset as the new workhouses were intended for healthy vagrants, a very different clientele than hungry and displaced communities. In 1847 a total of 130 workhouses were operating under varying degrees of strain. Half were full by December 1846 obliging the Guardians to adhere to legislation requiring them to refuse admission. Those who elected to provide food to unsuccessful applicants on humanitarian grounds were acting illegally until February 1847 when the Temporary Relief Act

permitted the allocation of cooked meals as part of the wider soup kitchen strategy.[91]

The rate of admissions to the North Dublin Union provided one index of the dimension of social pressure on the east coast. Whereas roughly fifty persons per week entered in October 1844, a range of eighty to 113 persons were admitted per week in October 1846. The institution was simply unequal to the escalating challenge on its doorstep and temporary additional 'workhouses' had to be inaugurated in the Linen Hall and Sheriff's Prison. Unsurprisingly, the meagre amelioration of accommodation was insufficient to safeguard the health of those taken off the streets. Overcrowding and the lack of segregation of the healthy from the sick all but ensured a 'fever' outbreak. Thirty Union residents were infected in May 1847 with a further eight smallpox and six scarlatina cases identified. As it proved impossible to transfer the ill to the teeming Fever Hospitals, a temporary hospital was opened in the inner suburb of Drumcondra which accepted close to 6,400 patients within a year. Such pragmatism may well have averted a major epidemic in the capital, but it contrasted with a general state of vacillation. As 1847 progressed, the national workhouse capacity was steadily increased and by late 1848 almost 150,000 could be admitted.[92]

Overall, the workhouses fulfilled their new mandate of housing and feeding Famine refugees with tolerable success for an environment devoid of long term co-ordination of state policy and finances. Assistance was certainly furnished with none of the delays and complicated paperwork which had stymied the public works. However, the co-existence of soup kitchens and 'indoor' workhouse relief was never intended. At its core, the Temporary Relief Act was an item of bridging legislation which authorised the

exercise of 'outdoor' relief prior to the introduction of the Poor Law Extension Act. The new act was conceived as a means of regulating direct provision of aid whilst safeguarding the traditional function of the workhouses. The downside of the reforms was that the burden of paying for relief was shifted from the Imperial Parliament to Irish ratepayers. Westminster planned for the scaling back of all relief in September and October 1847 when the return of the healthy potato crop was again predicted. A cursory reconnaissance of the type previously conducted annually by the Constabulary would have shown that such a harvest, even if blight-free, would be very small owing to the physical impossibility of planting sufficient seed. Instead, Trevelyan confounded informed Irish observers by using his enhanced authority to close the soup kitchens ahead of schedule between 15 and 29 August 1847. While the incidence of chronic mortality appeared to have slowed by then, mass deaths from starvation and related diseases remained very common.[93]

Fevers

The two most deadly fevers in 1847 were typhus, known also as 'black fever' or 'spotted fever', and relapsing fever, sometimes called 'yellow fever'. Both were carried by lice and, as such, endangered those massed on public works, soup kitchens and boarded in overcrowded workhouses. Other common afflictions included dysentery ('bloody flux'), tuberculosis, bronchitis and measles, all of which thrived in the oppressive climate of destitution. Starvation, when fatal, was generally described by medical authorities as 'famine dropsy' or 'hunger oedema', although the formal attribution of this cause of death was under recorded.

While lack of food was a major killer throughout the late 1840s, those in the early stages of starvation were highly vulnerable to chronic secondary afflictions due to the damage wrought by prolonged malnutrition on the immunity system. Disease frequently killed Famine victims before the relatively slow decline of starvation became terminal. Exposure killed able-bodied victims and rendered others susceptible to consumptive complaints, not least TB. Scurvy was also highly prevalent and was referred to at times as 'black leg' owing to the manner in which the victim's feet often presented the first visible signs of illness. It was noted by the Health Board that scurvy symptoms did not always retreat when the sufferer received food from the soup kitchens.[94]

The Central Board of Health which, incredibly, had been axed in August 1846, was urgently reconvened to grapple with the incipient fever epidemic of 1847. Between February 1847 and August 1850 the Board managed 373 hospitals specialising in the treatment and containment of fever. Timely intervention and extraordinary diversion of resources, such as £120,000 to acquire tents from the military, kept the latest crisis within bounds. For once common sense prevailed. Naturally, there was a degree of self-interest in containing the one facet of the Famine disaster which seriously threatened urban workforces for whom food was available. The arrival of fever-stricken refugees in Belfast and Dublin raised fears of contagion with healthy and skilled industrial workforces dying in large numbers. Thousands of fever victims were buried in a mass grave at Clifton Street Cemetery, Belfast. Families stranded in wretched hillside shacks could be quietly ignored whereas an influx of such persons into urban and middle-class

environments was an intolerable affront to social preten-
sions and the maintenance of economic equilibrium.

Anti-fever protection was necessarily uneven. In July
1847, 800 residents of Rooskey, Roscommon, contracted
disease without the benefit of access to hospitals or doc-
tors. The parish of Kilglass was particularly afflicted owing
to its unfortunate location midway between the relief committees of Elphin and Kilmore. Fr Henry Brennan attested
that 'fever has made its way into almost every house. The
poor creatures are wasting away and dying of want. In very
many instances the dead bodies are thrown in waste cabins
and dykes and are devoured by dogs. In some parts the
fields are bleached with the bones of the dead that were
previously picked by dogs'. Fr Brennan reported the potentially significant jurisdictional problem to Collett, MP for
Athlone and also to the new Viceroy, Earl Clarendon, without receiving acknowledgement. The last gambit of a direct
appeal to the British queen suggested itself to Brennan who
was ever concerned for 'the wants and tribulations of this
ill-fated portion of her Majesty's dominions'. The harsh fact
was that Kilglass parish was afforded no equivalency with
those of what the British Government regarded as the 'mai-
nland'.[95]

In some respects, George William Frederick Villiers
(Lord Clarendon) was placed in an impossible situation
when appointed Lord Lieutenant at short notice in May
1847. As with Peel, Clarendon knew Ireland better than
most English administrators and in 1827 had advised Lord
Anglessy during his term as Lord Lieutenant. From July
1846 Clarendon had served as President of the Board of
Trade under his colleague Russell and he was well versed
in the subtle intricacies of Anglo-Irish commerce. Catastrophe gripped the country in 1847 and the mindset adopted

in Westminster inflicted massive damage on a sector the government insisted was an integral part of the United Kingdom yet treated as a disfavoured colony. Clarendon was fully aware from his discussions with Wood that the economic situation in England would forestall the advancement of resources necessary to save the population from immiserisation and death. He had no answers for correspondents like Fr Brennan and no real power to wield through Dublin Castle. His hands were tied.

7. PRIVATE CHARITY

Death rates from starvation and fever would have been even higher if government efforts to safeguard the population had not been bolstered by private charity. Donations from Irish soldiers stationed in Calcutta had inspired the creation of the Indian Relief Fund in late 1845. In a amtter of weeks, £14,000 was raised and sent to Dublin from Calcutta and Bombay. A concurrent initiative in Boston grew out of the city's Repeal Association and, as such, also drew strength from the concern of politically-aware expatriates. However, international reportage of the Famine stimulated generous acts of charity outside the major Irish communities overseas. In New York, money was collected by Jewish, German Lutheran and Baptist congregations. The most celebrated assistance came from the Native Americans of the Choctaw Nation who subscribed $170 they could ill-afford following their recent expulsion from tribal lands to Oklahoma. In March 1847 Pope Pius IX issued an encyclical urging Catholics to assist the poor in Ireland through prayer and extraordinary cash donations. This proved important in that finances channelled through the Catholic network were sustained and continued into the later years of the Famine when donor exhaustion, distraction, disinterest and hostility reduced the scale of general subscriptions.

The single most important intervention was made by the Quakers who, at great cost in wealth and some in life, strove to fulfill their Christian duties by means of direct provision of aid. Joseph Bewley formed the Central Relief Committee of the Society of Friends in Dublin on 13 November 1846 which led to the establishment of an allied body in London shortly afterwards. Two prominent English

Quakers, William Edward Forster and James Hack Tuke, made a fact-finding tour to the west of Ireland during the Famine and published an account of their experiences as *A Visit to Connaught in the autumn of 1847*.[96] Forster, a native of Dorset was involved in the wool trade in Bradford and Chief Secretary of Ireland in 1880-82. He visited O'Connell in Derrynane in 1847 and refuted the allegations of estate mismanagement made by Foster and William Howard Russell of the *Times*. Forster's companion, Tuke, hailed from York and developed a life long interest in tackling the problems of rural Ireland. Tuke contracted fever in York in 1848 when assisting Irish immigrants, and encouraged by Forster, survived to play a notable role in the land reform issue in Ireland during the early 1880s. An advantageous connection was also formed between the Irish Relief Committee and Jacob Harvey who managed a major scheme of fundraising amongst America's sizeable Quaker communities.

Quaker charity financed privately-run soup kitchens, including the Cork centre in Barrack Street, which was favourably reported and depicted in the *London Illustrated News* of 16 January 1847. The simplicity, effectiveness and economy of Quaker operations did much to spur the Whig administration to underwrite a national, state-supported programme. Quaker-owned ironworks in Coalbrookdale, England, supplied fifty large boilers for the private soup kitchens in early 1847 and nearly 300 were provided during the Famine. Relief of this order undoubtedly saved thousands of lives, particularly as the Quakers were prepared to risk working in fever-stricken districts neglected by the Government. Several volunteer workers succumbed to fatal diseases and exhaustion, not least Bewley in Ireland and Harvey in the United States. They literally worked

themselves to death on behalf of the Irish poor. This effort continued until late 1847 when the Friends decided to withdraw from such intense activities in favour of indirect logistic support for long-term improvement. This step was partly owing to Quaker opposition to Poor Law reforms imposed by Westminster. Farm implements, seed and other practical commodities were distributed as the Government geared up its own soup kitchens and extended the functions of the workhouses. The unconditional nature of Quaker intervention earned them long-term respect in modern Ireland. This contrasted with the much resented and far lesser activities of some evangelical Protestants who made assistance contingent on conversion. In the century that followed those who had availed of this lifeline and converted were frequently derided as 'soupers' for having 'taken the soup'.

The void left by strategic disengagement of the Quakers was partly filled by American and Irish-American generosity. Senior political figures backed trans-Atlantic assistance, not least Vice-President George Mifflin Dallas who chaired an important meeting in Washington DC on 9 February 1847. Donations from the East Coast topped $1 million dollars by then with substantial sums flowing to Ireland from many American states. The Boston Relief Committee scored a major coup on St. Patrick's Day (17 March) 1847 when US Navy's *Jamestown* was loaded with supplies for Ireland. Congress had acceded to the overture of the Committee and authorised the dispatch of the *Jamestown*, followed by the *Macedonian*, to Ireland and Scotland respectively. The contribution of the British authorities was merely to waive import duties on the special freight. American hopes that London would be pressurised into more decisive responses proved illusory. The US Government had scored a moral victory using military vessels during

time of war against Mexico. Further official actions of this kind could not be made as they posed awkward diplomatic as well as practical issues.[97]

Two Irish agencies acted as focal points for international donations in 1846-7. In December 1846 the Central Relief Committee boasted members of the O'Connell and Fitzgerald families, as well as the ill-fated William Smith O'Brien MP of Dromoland, Limerick, who was transported to Van Diemen's Land (Tasmania, Australia) for sedition in October 1849. This broad spectrum of Irish political opinion, contrasted with the more select agenda of the Irish Relief Association. The Duke of Manchester, an Armagh magnate, was the driving force behind the Association and made no secret of his interest in exploiting the crisis to promote evangelical Protestantism. These substantial operations amassed sums of £42,000 and £63,000 respectively in 1846 which, in the case of the Committee, was distributed in the form of grants prior to the end of 1847. The fortunate recipients of aid were consequently able to buy otherwise unaffordable food. The Belfast General Relief Fund quickly amassed £4,000 after its foundation on 5 January 1847 but was criticised for spending the bulk in the west of Ireland instead of in the city where assistance was urgently required. Anglican Rev. Dr Thomas Drew and Presbyterian Rev. Dr John Edgar used the fund to further proselytising and temperance-linked missions in Connacht.[98]

This work was greatly boosted by the activities of the British Association for the Relief of the Extreme Distress in the Remote Parishes of Ireland which provided the considerable sum of £400,000 in 1847-8. The venture was conceived in London on 1 January 1847 by Munster man Stephen Spring Rice and the noted Jewish banker Baron Lionel de Rothschild. Earlier that day a correspondent of

the *Cork Examiner* stated: 'Not a single day passes by without abundant evidence of the total inadequacy of the present government, to wield the destinies of this great empire,
or to preserve from actual starvation the great majority of
this long misgoverned and unfortunate country'.[99]

Rothschild and Spring Rice attempted to fill as much of
the vacuum as possible with the charity of ordinary Britons.
They ostensibly sought to improve conditions in both Ireland and Scotland, a politically expedient but fictional
remit. The Scots, as all informed parties realised, had suffered hardship, but did not require substantial aid to preserve life. The vast bulk of the money raised was expended
in Connacht on the basis of the region's far greater need for
intervention. Major donors included Rothschild, whose
City of London offices were used to form the body, and the
Duke of Devonshire. They advanced £1,000 each to start
the fund whereas Charles Wood, a somewhat conflicted
personality whose professional stance at the Treasury
helped negate the prospect of decisive state funding, provided £400. A famous contribution of £2,000 was received
in the name of Queen Victoria whose advisors had been
embarrassed by Spring Rice into doubling the amount
originally intended. Perhaps the main benefit of this gesture was its legitimisation of Irish Famine relief during a
period in which coverage of the crisis in Britain was often
less than sympathetic.[100]

The Association envisaged direct engagement in Ireland
and secured the services of the Polish explorer and adven-
turer, Paul Edmunde, Count de Strzelecki. He had 'disco-
vered' and named Mount Kosciusko in New South Wales,
Australia, and was a high-profile and capable agent. When
in Ireland, Strzelecki oversaw the distribution of the British
money in the western counties where he formed an

extremely negative opinion of the country's landed gentry. He sought to assist children whenever possible and encountered problems when the Treasury, at Trevelyan's behest, objected to the scale of the Association's charitable actions. Nonetheless, the Association was providing food for an estimated 200,000 children in the western counties in 1848 when the Government was yet again reneging on its responsibilities. The Association was effectively wound up in the summer of 1848 when funding became a fraught issue exacerbated by Strzelecki's fractious relationship with Trevelyan. He returned to Britain without accepting payment for his work. Strzelecki's subsequent moral support for John Bright, the Rochdale Quaker, was one of the more lasting outcomes of the endeavour as it bolstered his advocacy of agrarian reform later enshrined in the Land Act of 1870. Writing of the Famine in January 1882, the Land League and Fenian leader Michael Davitt recalled: 'The charity of foreign nations was performing what Irish landlordism refused, with its usual brutal selfishness'.[101]

Exports and opinion

The unsettling paradox of produce being exported from a country afflicted with 'famine' whilst imports were received for commercial profit was not lost on the journalists of John Mitchel's *Nation*. On 12 June 1847 the paper reported the disquieting allegation that consignments of Irish food being sent to Le Harve, Bordeaux and Antwerp were 'meeting on the way cargoes of other corn arriving from Odessa, or Hamburg, or New York'. The key point was that, allowing for capitalist acumen, the Irish 'eventually got to eat' wheat which had been sold abroad for fifty shillings per quarter yet imported for eighty. In other words, while Irish

businessmen sold into the receptive, famine threatened and recovering economies of Western Europe in mid-1847, the incidence of starvation in their native country grew steadily.[102] Mitchel's followers held no truck with those who insisted that trade, however imbalanced, was necessary to sustain the healthy parts of the Irish economy through the worst crisis in living memory.

The reportage of the *Nation* may well have erred in specifics, but official figures for live cattle exports from Ireland record an increase from 186,483 head in 1846 to 201,811 in 1849. Sheep and lamb exports declined slightly from the substantial 259,257 animals to 241,061 for reasons unconnected with the Famine. Beef and mutton, of course, were too expensive for the starving Irish in 1847-8. Adequate wages could not then be obtained in either the private sector or in the discontinued public relief schemes. Pig exports, meanwhile, plummeted from 480,827 animals in 1846 to just 106,407 the following year. This collapse was attributed to the loss of the potato, the main feed of swine, but the grim fact that it was also the only animal widely available to the poor in 1845-6 suggests that pigs were sacrificed to prolong the survival of their owners. In some respects, the demise of the pigs paralleled that of the cottiers and labourers by whom they had once been tended. This subtext was as disconcerting as the buoyant exports of more valuable cattle and sheep. By 1849 a mere 68,053 pigs were embarked for slaughter abroad.[103]

Regardless of economic justifications, the export trade in grain and livestock challenged the conceptualisation of the Irish experience in terms of 'famine' occasioned by 'providence'. This, naturally, produced a visceral anger amongst informed contemporaries. In October 1847 an outraged resident of Macroom in Cork demanded: 'what will be done

with those two traffickers, the proselytiser and the corn merchant?'[104] Certainly, virtually nothing could be done from the benches of the House of Commons where William Smith O'Brien lambasted the Government in speech after speech without effect. In April, his conservative estimate that 240,000 had died of starvation failed to prevent a 20 per cent reduction in employment places on public works. As the most articulate and able Irish MP following the death of O'Connell in Genoa on 15 May 1847, Smith O'Brien was increasingly the channel through which Young Ireland addressed the British Establishment.[105]

The Famine was the catalyst though which Mitchel, James Fintan Lalor and Thomas Francis Meagher coalesced as an uncompromising hardcore within the once diffuse circles of Young Ireland. Closer to the republicanism of Wolfe Tone than their former backing for O'Connellism suggested, the militants gradually edged towards a position of espousing violent resistance. They joined the Irish Confederation which split from the Repeal Association on 13 January 1847 and used it as a vehicle to promote the cause of Irish self-determination. Significantly, the ascendancy of Young Ireland's militant tendency pre-dated the 'Year of Revolutions', 1848, when many proto-democrats and republicans struck for freedom in Europe. The increasing prominence of 'Meagher of the Sword' *et al* did not sit well with the lingering moderates whose early withdrawal from the Confederation in the course of 1847 ceded full control to the hardliners. Smith O'Brien functioned as the Confederate figurehead while Charles Gavan Duffy, another determined Repeal activist, worked in the wings. The engagement of such bourgeois and landed leaders owed much to their disaffection at Britain's maladministration of Ireland. The Famine crisis, in the context of positive

international precedents, was the prime factor in adding Ireland to the catalogue of European uprisings in 1848. Whereas independence had been a cherished if somewhat abstract objective of Young Ireland in 1845, by 1847 it seemed imperative for national survival.

The constitutional genesis of the Confederation rendered its leadership incapable of mobilising mass support in 1847. Reformist orientated ideology could not be fully reconciled with revolutionary methodology and unanimity was never achieved in this regard. Lacking paramilitary organisation and equipment, the prospect of emulating the United Irishmen, or even the less sophisticated Defenders and Ribbonmen, diminished with every passing month. The vigilance of Dublin Castle and rapidly declining health of those from whose ranks a popular army must be recruited ensured that a protest in arms was the most that could be realistically envisaged. Armed opposition to illegal evictions was also possible and this was advocated by Mitchel and Meagher. Ideally, Duffy and Smith O'Brien hoped for a bloodless 'coup' in which Westminster would cede its authority and tolerate a friendly democratic regime in Dublin. The unhappy experience in England of their Chartist ally, Feargus O'Connor, did not dampen their misplaced optimism. In the event, no serious unilateral action was taken in 1847 when the Confederates built up their networks as best they could and bided their time.[106]

Crime and outrage, November 1847

The assassination of Major Denis Mahon of Strokestown Park House, Roscommon, was probably the most discussed death of the Famine.[107] Mahon was in the process of eradicating conacre from his recently acquired estate of

9,000 acres and had invested £4,000 transporting 800 unwanted tenants to Canada in 1847. This programme, ironically, was viewed as laudable and progressive by his peers, although it was undertaken with a view to evading the greater costs of maintaining the poor in Roscommon workhouse. Around 25 per cent of the assisted migrants on the *Virginius* died en route to Quebec and news of their fate steeled others to resist when Mahon sought to dispatch them in their wake. When various inducements failed to clear the land of its inhabitants, Mahon responded by evicting 600 families totaling 3,000 tenants. This proved a deadly error. He was accosted by two men and shot dead on 2 November 1847 when making his way home from a meeting of the Board of Guardians in Roscommon Town. This discriminate and well-planned attack was a classic act of Ribbonism and all the more unsettling for Irish conservatives as a result. Many would have drawn disquieting inferences from the open celebration of Mahon's killing with the lighting of bonfires. Very little information of value was procured in relation to the identity of the assailants. Mahon, like many of his peers, had sat for a formal portrait. This appealling image of an officer in his prime was made available for posthumous dissemination and he quickly became a symbol of latent threat posed by the restive Irish.[108]

False allegations by Lord Farnham that the local Catholic parish priest had marked Mahon for death from the pulpit unleashed a flurry of bigoted statements. In actuality, Fr Michael McDermott had simply criticised Mahon at a meeting of the Strokestown Relief Committee for being absent in London while his tenants starved.[109] Archbishop John MacHale of Tuam immediately responded with a robust defence that surprised many for its unusually strong tone and language. MacHale recalled the execution of his parish

priest for assisting the French expeditionary forces of General Jean Humbert in Connacht in 1798 and had braved the same risk as a boy running messages for the United Irishmen. He would not accept a felon setting campaign of innuendo against Fr McDermott in 1847 whether emanating from Farnham, an Orange Peer, or several addled English Catholics.

MacHale's stance on the Mahon controversy confirmed the new-found confidence of the Catholic Hierarchy, which had already confronted Young Ireland over the Colleges Act. The bishops, unlike the pluralist republicans, did not welcome 'godless' colleges in which the Catholic perspective on education was absent. With O'Connell dead in May 1847 and his former Repeal associates in disarray, senior Catholic religious figures were increasingly disposed to represent their sectional interests directly. If generally supportive of the political status quo, the bishops gave the majority underclass of Irish Catholics a far stronger voice outside Parliament than was possible within its precincts. Militancy arising from the dire experience of Famine impelled the Catholic revival in its aftermath.[110]

Violent incidents flared in the winter of 1847-8 when many rate collectors and landlords were attacked by desperate tenants. The Crime and Outrage (Ireland) Bill came before the House of Commons on 29 November 1847 and was enacted with royal assent on 20 December. While lacking the explicit intent of the infamous Insurrection Act, the new legislation was intended to inhibit the killings of Irish landowners. Youths and men living in the vicinity of fatal crimes were threatened with two years imprisonment if they failed to assist investigations. This implied that the civil authorities in Ireland were incapable of safeguarding the landed elite by conventional means. The Irish

Constabulary, a body without equivalent in England, had existed since 1836 as a fully-armed, national force in almost 9,000 barracks. If powerless to protect those regarded as enemies of the people, the constabulary were called upon to enforce the prohibition on possession of firearms by those not entitled to the privilege. Legislation of this kind had never deterred Irish agrarian insurgents from targeting perceived oppressors and one of the most important aspects of the Crime and Outrage Act was that it led to an additional 5,000 soldiers being sent to Limerick city, Arklow and Clonmel. This accretion of military strength may or may not have been strictly necessary in view of Ireland's general state as a heavily garrisoned society but it reassured nervous landlords that the government empathised with their situation.

Late 1847: Gregory Clause and evictions

The closure of public schemes and soup kitchens marked a retreat from direct provision of state aid, which was by no means offset by the voiding of notional debts owed by one part of the civil service to another. Moreover, the employment of subsidised labour on capital projects benefited transport infrastructure in Ireland at a time when the logic of such work was illustrated by parallel investment in railway construction nationwide. The retreat from public works, however, was linked to a concerted attack. Russell insisted that the Irish Poor Law framework assume the entire burden of relief from the Treasury and required that a rate of five shillings in the pound be levied. Landlords were thus obliged to pay a set amount per tenant on their estate. This was an aggressive strategy in which the collection of

£1 million from rate payers was achieved using intimidation and coercion. As before, it was assumed in London that there was no salient reason why the Irish tax payers should not shoulder the costs of alleviating the distress of the Irish poor. No account was taken of the dysfunctional nature of landlord/tenant relations in Ireland and the exploitation of this imbalanced nexus by British importers. Many Irish landlords were severely financially pressured by rent defaulters and a small minority was victimised. Twelve were assassinated in 1847 which, although aberrant, was remarkably few given that over 3,500 impoverished families had been evicted in 1846 and 6,000 in 1847. This death toll compared with the early phase of the 'Tithe War' in 1830-32 when 242 landlords, proctors and agents were killed. Such turmoil was unknown in England where a more equitable system of leasing and a generally stable economy benefited landlord and tenant.[111]

The final form of the Poor Law Extension Act was hammered out in the House of Commons in the months preceding its eventual promulgation on 8 June 1847. Sections of the Act addressed Irish concerns, while others were designed to minimise the impact of such factors on the British economy. The inflow of refugees into British ports struck press and parliamentary commentators as a testament to the failure of Irish landlords who were already held in contempt for their alleged evasion of responsibility and exploitation of relief schemes. In short, the Extension Act promised to hold the Irish poor within the catchments of their native Poor Law Unions. The Irish rate payer, rather than the British tax system, would render assistance. Having recognised the limitations of the beleaguered workhouses, legal provision was made for the Unions to administer temporary 'outdoor' aid to those who could not be

granted admission. This, however, massively increased the financial strain of the Guardians appointed to manage the Unions. They were enjoined to extract the necessary funds from rates alone. Guardians who did not press landlords for unpaid rates were subject to dismissal and the mechanism of discharging such persons was refined. Scrutiny was entrusted to Edward Twistleton, head of the new Poor Law Commission in Dublin. Ominously, the Act permitted Guardians to buy land for burial plots adjacent to the work-houses in order to relieve pressure on standard graveyards. Death rates in workhouses had attained levels which public cemeteries could not absorb.

Irish landlords vehemently opposed the thrust of the legislation because it threatened to squeeze them finan-cially. Although powerless to prevent its implementation, they lobbied for and won a significant amendment in the 'Gregory' or 'Quarter-acre' clause. William Gregory, a prof-ligate Galway landlord and conservative MP for Dublin City, forcefully argued the interests of his class in the House of Commons and gave his name to one of the most infa-mous amendments in Irish legal history. Only two Irish MPs, including Smith O'Brien, recognised the danger posed by this amendment and voted accordingly. The 'Gre-gory Clause' denied workhouse entry to those who farmed plots larger than a quarter acre, regardless of the condition of the property or its inhabitants. This was a considerable proportion of the population given that over 135,000 Irish farms were smaller than one acre in 1844.[112] While ostensi-bly intended to ensure that only those in dire want solicited admission, the real value of the clause was its utility to land-lords in evicting small holding tenants who had fallen into arrears with rent. All such persons were required to surren-der their property and, therefore, cease to burden landlords

intent on re-aggrandising their estates. In practice, those seeking Famine relief after June 1847 were virtually certain to face eviction, including small farmers who had weathered the storms of 1845 and 1846 only to collapse in the relentless face of 'Black 47'.

Generally, families forced to abandon their plots had their cottages levelled or otherwise rendered uninhabitable by the agents of the landlords. There was no political will to police this illegal, but widespread, phenomenon and Home Secretary Sir George Grey discounted the notion of prosecuting offending landlords in March 1848. This was a somewhat surprising abnegation as illegal estate clearances totally subverted the real purpose of the Extension Act by diverting evicted tenants into the rate supported Poor Law Unions. However, Russell's cabinet included men like Viscount Palmerstown, the Irish Foreign Secretary, who blatantly admitted that land reform 'necessarily implies a long continued and systematic ejectment of smallholders and of squatting cottiers'.[113] Sensibly, many landlords wanted to increase the size of rented farms, convert tillage estates to pasture and recoup financial losses accruing from the Famine. Removing inconvenient tenants was a means to such ends and illegal methods of doing so were all too common. Russell lacked the moral courage to ensure that those within his cabinet would promote observance of the law by Irish landlords. Thus hamstrung, the Prime Minister was unlikely to prevail with the demurring Grey who numbered Wood and Trevelyan amongst his closest colleagues. Indeed, Trevelyan in his 1848 publication *The Irish Crisis*, re-emphasised the primacy of the landowning classes whose local insight he believed was 'a powerful motive' to effectively manage relief they had partly funded.[114]

Far from spurring Irish landowners to more responsible estate management, the 'Quarter acre' amendment enabled the gentry to rid themselves of unwanted tenants. While this outcome won favour with economists and undoubtedly benefited many landlords, the methodology employed seemed unduly harsh in the context of a famine. With no automatic right of return from the workhouse, the misery of homelessness was added to that of starvation and destitution. Many distressed families starved *in situ* rather than cast themselves permanently adrift. They suffered, in consequence, a public and shocking demise. Other tenants negotiated terms with landlords under which they voluntarily destroyed their own roofs in return for permission to recycle the discarded beams and thatch into flimsy bivouacs. Harrowing reports of innumerable tragedies discomforted elements of British liberal opinion and it was privately acknowledged by Russell that the 'Gregory Clause' was little more than an instrument of landlord tyranny.[115]

The Government was reluctantly obliged to change tack, primarily as the misapplication of the Act proved uneconomic owing to its knock-on effect on rate levies. From May 1848 it was possible to receive outdoor relief even if still in occupation of a quarter acre site. However, additional clauses that would have significantly curbed evictions and protected tenants were rejected in the House of Lords. As before, civil and military protection was provided to the most prolific evictors, but denied to those illegally dispossessed. In fact, those who resisted eviction risked imprisonment whereas offending bailiffs and landlords were effectively indemnified. The *Tipperary Vindicator* touched on potentially explosive allegations in December 1848 when it claimed: 'the work of undermining

the population is going on stealthily, but steadily … more deadly than the plague. We do not say that there exists a conspiracy to uproot the 'mere Irish' but we do aver, that the fearful system of wholesale ejectment, of which we daily hear, and which we daily behold, is a mockery of the eternal laws of God-a flagrant outrage on the principles of nature. Whole districts are cleared … There are vast tracts of the most fertile land in the world in this noble county now thrown out of tillage. No spade, no plough goes near them … a demon, with all the vindictive passions by which alone a demon can be influenced, is let loose and menaces destruction'.[116]

Serious damage had been incurred by Ireland's small holders prior to Russell's pusillanimous attempt to recover the situation. Exposure joined 'famine fever' as a major killer of the Irish poor and remained a concern for those discharged from the workhouses into the early 1850s. From December 1848 the plight of the impoverished and unsheltered was compounded by an outbreak of 'Asiatic cholera'. This virile killer of the infirm spread from the Continent via Britain to Ireland with deadly effect until the disease retreated in July 1849. The Irish epidemic was incorrectly traced to a man deported to Belfast from Scotland, but was actually already present in the city's slums. At least 30,000 deaths were directly attributed to cholera in Ireland 1849, some of which would very probably have occurred in any case due to starvation and the more common diseases.[117]

8. YOUNG IRELAND AND THE RISING OF 1848

The Irish Confederate faction of Young Ireland observed the events of late 1847 and early 1848 with a realisation that they would have to either secure victory or accept forcible dissolution. At this low ebb, matters took a turn for the better on the Continent. The French Revolution that deposed Louis Phillipe in late February 1848 was achieved with such ease that even the habitually cautious Smith O'Brien and Gavan Duffy explored the possibility of making stronger demands of the British government. French success emboldened the more animated Meagher and Mitchel to discard the cherished goal of Repeal in favour of a sovereign Republic. The compelling role of the Famine in suggesting this path was clear from their writings, which urged Irishmen to resist eviction, withhold rents, refuse to pay rates and procure arms. Subsequent public statements and the appearance of additional inflammatory articles in United Irishman by various Confederates forced the hand of the authorities. Meagher, Mitchel and Smith O'Brien were arrested in Dublin on 2 March 1848 following a meeting in which Meagher proposed giving London an ultimatum on the creation of an Irish Republic. He stated: 'if the constitution opens to us no path to freedom … it will be our duty to fight'.[118]

Legal proceedings failed to convict Smith O'Brien and Meagher of sedition but on 26 May 1848 their colleague Mitchel was sentenced to fourteen years transportation. His conviction under the draconian Treason Felony Act, which had only become law on 22 April, signalled that the Government was prepared to engineer whatever contingencies

it deemed necessary to quash dissent. Lesser agitators were also then pursued. Mitchel's ordeal followed an important statement by the Catholic hierarchy on 21 April in which the monarch was warned of the danger of insurrection arising from Famine desperation yet assured of the church's continued loyalty to the crown. This lessened the moral authority of agitators who claimed to act on the part of the people and the conservative line of the clergy was graphically reinforced during the abortive 'June Days' revolt in Paris when more than a thousand people perished. The cumulative effects of such events strengthened Clarendon's ability and resolve to forestall the uprising anticipated during the late summer of 1848. Several Confederate leaders were detained on 8-11 July and their printed organs were suppressed one by one. Kevin Izod O'Doherty, Young Irelander and surgical assistant at the County of Dublin's Fever Hospital, was imprisoned in Newgate for publishing an allegedly seditious article in the Irish Tribune. It proclaimed: 'Every ditch has its corpse, and every lording Moloch his hetacomb of murdered tenantry. Clearly we are guilty if we turn not our hand against the enemies of our race'.[119] Gavan Duffy of the Nation, a man with a far higher but less incendiary profile, joined O'Doherty in the city prison on 9 July.

At this low ebb the bailed Meagher illustrated the potential for protest on 16 July by leading 20,000 supporters into his native Waterford city. The Government moved first and with decision on 18 July when martial law was proclaimed in Dublin, Waterford, Cork and Drogheda. This extraordinary step was followed on 22 July with the suspension of *habeas corpus*, a clear cut expression of policy which contrasted with Westminster's confused handling of the Famine. The military was poised to act against those who

took arms illegally and any prisoners taken could be held for long periods without trial. The Rising of 1848 was not so much defeated as pre-empted. Clarendon successfully dictated its timing and while it is inherently unlikely that the crackdown was influenced by news that the potato crop of 1848 was diseased, the predicted response of Young Ireland neutralised their long term potential.

From 22 July 1848 Meagher's clique faced into a possible revolt with a divided and partially-imprisoned amateur leadership and an unknown number of prospective followers who lacked training, chain of command, weaponry or instructions. The fact that the countryside was ravaged with starvation and disease was hardly propitious. Ireland was particularly well garrisoned in 1848 in order to protect the grain economy and landlords and there was no question of surprising a Government which had already commenced counter-insurgency initiatives. At the last minute Fr John Kenyon, formerly a belligerent and effective organiser in North Tipperary, declined to add his considerable authority to the enterprise. This ruined any chance of linking a Kilkenny/ Waterford zone of influence to the Limerick sector and beyond. Under such unremittingly negative circumstances, the reasonable level of mobilisation achieved by Young Ireland in the week following 29 July 1848 was indicative of deep-seated unrest.

Meagher, for one, knew that a purely military victory was impossible. However, a token armed showing by Young Ireland would focus national and international attention on the Irish crisis. With this modest objective in mind he took pains to avoid armed actions in Dublin where he believed a doomed if 'desperate fight' was inevitable.[120] Major bloodshed without the prospect of triumph was anathema to Meagher, just as the wholesale destruction of

private property troubled Smith O'Brien. Matters might have taken a more violent course had mid-ranking leaders such as James Stephens and Michael Doheny exercised high command. Indeed, Mitchel, then awaiting transportation, had intended to rise in Dublin for precisely the reason Meagher demurred. On moving through Wexford into Kilkenny and Tipperary, the rebels who rallied with whatever firearms they had to hand were generally well received. Thousands joined the leaders in the Comeragh Mountains and other inaccessible locations. If far from a powerful tide of insurgency, the rebels established that they were capable of traversing distances without being contained or defeated by the superior firepower of the authorities. This required the linked factors of popular acceptance short of participation and Government indisposition to force large scale confrontations.

The best-known event of the Rising occurred on 29 July at Farrenrory, near Ballingarry, Tipperary. Smith O'Brien's column failed to overcome a small but well-armed force of constables who had taken refuge in the McCormack farmhouse. In a characteristic, but naïve, move, Smith O'Brien attempted to besiege rather than assault the defenders and thereby invited an immediate turning of the tables. Greater militancy was displayed elsewhere with attacks on three police barracks in Kilkenny and various menacing probes in the vicinity of Carrick-on-Suir and Waterford. Significantly, no major clashes occurred between any of the Young Ireland groups which roamed Munster at will and the strong military forces available to the Commander-in-Chief, Field Marshall Sir Edward Blakeney. The Young Irelanders were permitted to vent their anger in a less than determined manner that posed no threat to the security of the state. Very few prisoners were taken in view of the

numbers engaged and casualties were exceptionally light due to the lack of combat.

The Rising of 1848, in virtually every respect, was a protest rather than an attempted revolution. As such it has a tenuous claim to a place in the republican continuum of 1803 and 1867. This reality permitted leniency and the compromised leaders were all spared execution, notwithstanding the ritual imposition of death sentences at Clonmel in September 1848. The main figures were deported to Van Diemen's Land by July 1849 where they were well treated upon arrival. If they were taken aback by the transportation of a fellow MP to an Australian penal colony, there was little in the business of Westminster to indicate understanding of his cause. The Rising angered the misinformed British public and may well have contributed to the decline in charitable donations towards Famine relief.[121]

Charles Greville, clerk of the Privy Council, was astounded by what he regarded as the effrontery and 'madness of the people' in Ireland. He surmised: 'The Irish will look in vain to England, for no subscription or parliamentary grants or aid of any sort, public or private, will they get; the sources of charity and benevolence are dried up; the current which flowed last year has been effectually choked by the brutality and ingratitude of the people, and the rancorous fury and hatred with which they have met our exertions to serve them. The prospect, neither more nor less than that of civil war and famine, is dreadful, but it is unavoidable'. It must have been difficult for Greville to reconcile this deep sense of betrayal with the day to day responsibilities of Executive Government.[122]

9. 'DISTRESSED' UNIONS

Despite the pretense of management oversight and a notionally uniform relief policy, the Unions operated without logic or consistency. Many workhouses admitted all manner of applicants, including 'impotent poor' dependents of able-bodied adults, whereas some Guardians were more restrictive. Securing food and shelter, therefore, was generally, but not always, dependent on the availability of workhouse accommodation. In December 1846, Quaker activist James Tuke had found that Carrick-on-Shannon workhouse in Leitrim had room for 700 but admitted only 280.[123] Admission was less important in cases where the Guardians authorised outdoor relief. Tralee workhouse, Kerry, was attacked on 5 November 1847 when a crowd flying a black flag attempted to force access having been refused outdoor relief. The military and police were required to clear the premises when the main gate was smashed.[124] At Lismore Union, Waterford, it was claimed in December that 'week after week, the trembling skeletons of human beings are denied relief, there being no room in the Workhouse'. The chairman of its Board of Guardians was the reputedly 'high-minded' ultra-loyalist Sir Richard Musgrave, who withheld sustenance from those denied entry.[125] Chance factors such as local demography and location of the workhouse, circumstances that bore little or no relation to the incidence of Famine, attained crucial significance in shaping admission and relief practices.

If admitted, stone breaking, capstan turning and other forms of debilitating hard labour was demanded of some inmates to prove destitution. Others were not tested. Rations distributed in outdoor relief mode could be

cooked, raw or a mixture of both and were delivered to recipients either daily or weekly. The condition of food had profound consequences for those obliged to travel on foot with a perishable, life-saving commodity. Food was usually given free upon application but could be sold below cost price to those deemed to possess the means. Guardians could either manage the distribution themselves or subcontract the task to shopkeepers and other agents. In short, the whim of the Guardians was a major determinant in terms of who lived and who died. If restrained to a degree by the threat of ignominious dismissal, this sanction was typically imposed on men who had shown insufficient zeal in collecting rates from neighbouring landlords. Fiscal mismanagement was frowned upon but there were no penalties or admonishments for failing to keep their clientele alive.

The steady growth of workhouses, all but dictated by the primacy of Poor Law relief as delineated in the Extention Act, continued into 1849. Bed capacity rose from 150,000 to 250,000. Moreover, the continuance of Famine conditions obliged more and more to fulfill the secondary role as dispensaries of outdoor relief. By 1848 almost half of all Unions were giving food to all applicants while a mere twenty-five of 131 Unions still discriminated. In April 1848, the North Dublin Union alone assisted 3,300 residents whilst feeding 6,500 per week in outdoor relief.[126] By early July 1849, 784,000 persons were in receipt of outdoor relief and the upwards trend continued as new Unions were created to cope with unprecedented demand. A total of 163 Poor Law Unions had been formalised by 1850 under the auspices of the Lord Lieutenant, Chief Secretary, Assistant Chief Secretary and Chief Commissioner who collectively comprised the new Irish Commission. The exponential increase in numbers gravely unbalanced an already

precarious Union economy which the Commission was required to administer. Consequently, the most powerful political coterie in Ireland, an unelected and generally English body, controlled a system of poor relief which Irish MPs had campaigned to defeat.[127]

Rate-in-Aid, 1849

The concentration of extreme suffering in Connacht, Munster and south Ulster highlighted the fact that workhouses, originally sited with a view to reducing vagrancy in the thirty-two counties, were at best an imperfect mechanism to administer large-scale relief. Finance was the Achilles heel as it was clearly impossible for the worst affected regions to set, let alone collect, rates at levels that would have met their outgoings. Total co-operation of solvent landlords was never forthcoming and many were actively using the 'Gregory Clause' to dispossess tenants of holdings which they were otherwise liable to pay partial or full rates. Guardians were placed in an invidious situation and twenty-two 'distressed' Unions were running at a serious deficit by the early summer of 1849. With mounting arrears and little prospect of the Unions ever repaying Government loans, the stratagem of 'Rate-in-Aid' was implemented.

Essentially, 'Rate-in-Aid' was an extraordinary additional levy of 6d in the pound which was collected in June 1849. A second and final levy of 2d in the pound was imposed in December 1849. Whereas all Irish electoral divisions paid the levies, the cash raised was diverted to the bankrupt Unions of the west and south. This *de facto* special subsidy contravened Poor Law regulations, as well as Whig financial principles. The announcement of the policy was

accompanied by an upfront commitment of £50,000 of a proposed £100,000 in matching funds towards what was intended as a debt clearance drive. A fund of £434,365 was thus created.[128] This much needed grant blurred the critical fact that Irish taxpayers were being compelled to pay for Famine relief in preference to the Imperial Treasury. London's approach signalled that the crisis was still officially considered as a purely domestic matter for Ireland. Bracing landowners implied that their willful neglect had been judged deleterious to the situation. This was partly true. Yet, no notion of culpability on the part of Dublin Castle or Westminster was entertained and, with ruthless consistency, no meaningful financial liability was accepted. Irish Nationalists naturally queried the value of membership of a United Kingdom and Empire constituted under such terms.

Twistleton of the Irish Poor Law Commission was appalled by Westminster's stance and resigned in protest. His parting shot in March 1849 condemned the 'indifference of the House of Commons' in pursuing 'a policy that must be one of extermination'.[129] This may have struck some of his English associates as unduly harsh but Twistleton knew that an average of 2,700 Irish people died every week from Famine-related causes and that 'Rate-in-Aid' was a monumental evasion of responsibility.[130] Clarendon, equally discomforted, feared violent repercussions which did not materialise. Isaac Butt, no firebrand in 1849, had two years previously expressed frustration as to how 'if, bearing our share of all imperial burdens-when calamity falls upon us we are to be told that we then recover our separate existence as a nation'.[131] Peel was similarly perplexed in 1849 and argued, ineffectually, that the Irish Poor Law should be modified yet again to incorporate the best practices and protections offered under the English model.

In Belfast, where the cholera epidemic had commenced in December 1848, the Poor Law Guardians rallied to protect local class interests by making false assertions in early 1849 that the industry of the north-east was supporting the idleness of the west. In fact, Leinster Unions carried a heavier rate load than those of the Belfast sector and the 'conditional loyalty' of certain Ulster MPs was noted in the Commons by a Dublin MP.[132]

The clinical refinancing of consolidated debts revealed that belief in *laissez-faire* had survived a series of Whig legislative blunders. Repayment of almost £4 million of non-remitted Government relief loans was pursued by London until 1853, at which time they were theoretically written off in exchange for additional customs and income taxes. As with costs arising from the cessation of the sectarian Tithe in 1838, a belated measure of reform was presented as if it were a magnanimous gesture. In actuality, Westminster had simply changed the method of extracting its dividend from both Irish tithes and Famine loans. Imposing duties on Irish spirits exports to Britain in 1853 was nakedly opportunistic, to say the least, and not calculated to assist the long road to economic recovery. Given that the typical annual tax return of the British Government in the 1840s exceeded £50 million, it was patently absurd to argue that Westminster could ill-afford Famine relief in Ireland. Around £8.1 million of state finances was diverted to Ireland in 1845-50 and this expenditure included cash which had been levied in the first instance from Irish rate-payers who ultimately bore the brunt of all relief. An abuse of power of this magnitude might be overlooked if simply a matter of fiscal wrangling within the corridors of power but the price of 1.1. million Irish dead was too high to be discounted. Twistleton had

made much the same point in alluding to the money wasted on prosecuting the Caffre War.

The British reading and voting public was routinely mis-informed as to the modest extent of Westminster's financial aid to Ireland in the late 1840s. Ignorance rendered them ill-equipped to equate this supposed benevolence with the persistent lack of signs of improvement in Ireland. The Famine appeared endemic by 1848 when it was maintained that British largesse of 1845-7 had been squandered. Unsound and facile explanations of this phenomenon were offered which, in the case of the *Times* and *Punch*, often entailed racially charged comments on the imagined life-styles of Irish Catholics. Savage caricatures of 'Celts' con-trasted with normal depictions of 'Britons' to seed a myth of a hapless, parasitic and pre-modern underclass reaping the whirlwind of its own atavism. It was not coincidental that such propaganda served to reinforce imperialist delusions of cultural supremacy. The near bloodless Rising of 1848, moreover, enabled hostile reporters to highlight the per-ception of the Irish as disloyal and dangerous. Richard Doyle, a leading *Punch* illustrator during the Famine, was not only Irish but a religious Catholic. His cover design was used for over a century even though he resigned from the publication in 1850 when he discerned that the veil of satire was being used to cover the sectarianism and racism of the editors.[133]

The comparison of Irish degeneracy and English decency dovetailed neatly with fashionable views of 'mora-lism', which ascribed social problems to the immutable, innate flaws of those beset. Given the established status of the Anglican community, it was hardly surprising that there were also frequent allusions to the esoteric concept of 'providentialism', particularly in view of the evangelical

revivalism which had enthralled Trevelyan and many other decision makers. Even the comparatively fair-minded *Illustrated London* News, a purveyor of more honest copy and generic images, erred in magnifying the virtues of English tax payers. The net result of this anti-Irish media was the elevation of the non-aristocratic Briton at the expense of the Irish Celt. Scottish Celts derived a modicum of reflected glory on the spurious premise that they, unlike their Irish counterparts, had extricated themselves from Famine. It was obviously not considered that the pro-Scottish bias shown by Trevelyan in 1846 weakened this thesis. Any prospect of Irish MPs receiving a proper hearing in the House of Commons was undermined by a wall of bad journalism and the ill-conceived outrage it engendered.

It is generally believed that Britain's emergent school of classical economists exerted little influence on Whig policy formation on Ireland during the Famine. If so, it was not for want of effort and key elements of their economic philosophy were enshrined in decisions taken by the Treasury. In 1847 Nassau Senior used Swiftian malevolence to execrate the agricultural structure of the country in his *The differences between Ireland and England.* The statistics, retrospective observations and pseudo-scientific comparisons revealed a weak grasp of Irish social conditions, culture and politics. The author was, however, a long term Hibernophobe and, unlike Malthus, a veteran lobbyist of English policy makers on the issue. If unsuccessful in urging Russell's bureaucrats to steer the course to a full Irish agricultural revolution, Senior's populist diatribe performed an interim service by endorsing the pre-conceived notions of English superiority which mandated the project. His influence may be confined to a mere patriotic reaffirmation of British forms, yet valid criticisms underlie parts of his

invective and it is impossible to gauge the reception of the rational and irrational content. Senior and other professional economists colluded with the Establishment by exonerating them of their failure to regulate Ireland's malfunctioning landlord/tenant relationship.

Russell had a long association with Senior who in April 1836 addressed a notionally 'confidential' document to him criticising the *Third Report from the Commissioners for Inquiring into the condition of the poor in Ireland*. The economist then identified the Whiteboys as a significant impediment to agricultural development in Ireland and attributed 'much of the turbulence of that population to the want of occupation for a great portion of their time'.[134] Starvation nullified Whiteboyism, at least in its traditional form, and this demise held out the prospect of faster-paced land reform in the late 1840s. Senior, Peel and Russell concurred on the necessity of anglicising Ireland and, if the question of how best this was to be attained permitted debate, the food crisis was recognised as a highly useful lever. Archbishop Richard Whately was privately informed by Senior in April 1847 that the disaster had left two million more people in Ireland than was required for the new economy envisaged. He was then unsuccessfully lobbying against outdoor relief on the grounds that it was unsafe to administer aid in that form due to the attendant security risks of massing large groups of impoverished and unsettled persons. Social control remained a major pre-occupation of the economist. In this respect the limited reach of Senior's clique may have prevented even higher excess mortality rates in Ireland.[135]

Encumbered estates, 1848-1849

The persistence of Famine and economic stress faced by hundreds of Irish landlords forced the pace of change in rural Ireland. Russell's insistence that relief be financed by the Irish Poor Law and the rates which sustained it drove thousands of landowners into bankruptcy. Well-managed, profitable and fertile estates were capable of withstanding the Famine at its most severe. This was the case with the Devonshire estates of Bandon, Cork, and Lismore, Waterford, where the ratio of rents collected and rates paid remained healthy in the midst of national crisis. This was untypical, as was the comparatively good heath of the tenants. Resident landlords or effective middlemen and agents were often a factor in maintaining solvency and part of the logic underpinning Smith O'Brien's vain attempts to have absentee landlords subjected to a punitive tax. Most estates, especially in the hard-hit west and south of Ireland, were exposed to serious strain by the food supply crisis, notwithstanding the short lived experiment of 'Rate-in-Aid'.

The fixture of the £4 property valuation as the threshold for landlord rate obligations to the Unions remained a major incentive to evict under the 'Gregory Clause'. Unsurprisingly, the dulling of this incisive tool by additional clauses did not stem the tide of legal evictions, which rose with every year of the Famine until 1850. Repossession figures remained very high into the mid-1850s as the national population continued to plummet. Tens of thousands of those ejected during the Famine were permitted to return to their farms upon paying arrears and large numbers were readmitted as 'caretakers' without settling their debts. They jointly comprised a minority totaling 48,000 in 1849-50. At least 72,000 were permanently evicted in 1849 and a further

74,000 in 1850. Over 102,000 more people were formally evicted by the end of 1853. This amounted to approximately 49,000 families driven off the land since 1849 when the Famine was receding in most sectors. This stark numerical imprint of tragedy excludes vast numbers of illegal land dispossessions, as well as abandonment arising from emigration, migration and death.[136]

Westminster was not entirely unmoved by this disquieting exodus. Kilrush Union, County Clare, became the focus of a House of Commons enquiry under the progressive George Poulett Scrope MP. Upon detailed investigation it was established in July 1850 that two landlords, Colonel Crofton Vandeleur and Marcus Keane, had been the prime offenders in evicting over 14,000 people in a single west Clare Union. Availing of police protection, Keane had levelled over 500 houses in the vicinity of the coast where some sectors lost around 75% of their population as a result.[137] In May 1849 Vandeleur had appeared before Sir John Young's Select Committee on the Irish Poor Law to praise the 'wonderful' manner in which the inmates of Kilrush workhouse had borne their privations. He described how in December 1847 'at least 3,000 people came to the workhouse' seeking 'more extended out-door relief' and were rebuffed with the assistance of the military. When pressed by G. C. Lewis on the related issue of evictions in the Union the Colonel acknowledged that there had been 'a large number' owing to 'nonpayment of rent, and the 4 L rating clause'. He admitted that the dwellings were levelled 'except where the farms were of a certain size, and where another tenant was put into it; but the class of tenants that has been lately evicted is that class of cottier tenants where their homes were worth nothing, but were an incumbrance upon the land'.[138]

Yet clearing off unwanted tenants was no panacea for landlords. They were hampered by the difficulty in finding suitable replacements and also in deriving adequate compensation for the seizure or 'distraint' of tenant possessions in lieu of rent arrears. The Whig Government strenuously opposed special loans for failing estates even as they professed displeasure at the level of illegal evictions which mushroomed in consequence. No allowance was made for humane landlords who incurred private debts in order to create paid labour for their tenants or to furnish them directly with charity. Instead, the Government combated the threatened implosion of the agrarian sector by means of the Encumbered Estates Act of 1848 and its sequel in July 1849. Irish agricultural exports were simply too valuable to the British economy to be allowed become a casualty of the Famine. From a Whig perspective, the reduction of tillage acreage in Ireland and increase in live cattle exports were encouraging signs of progress.

The Acts created an Encumbered Estates Court which first convened in Dublin in 24 October 1849. This was replaced four years later by a Landed Estates Court when the still faltering economics of Ireland guaranteed much business. The Courts oversaw the sale of mortgaged and otherwise failed estates and managed the settlement of outstanding debts with creditors. Given that the inhabitants of the estates in question were effectively bereft of constitutional protection, there was no mechanism to prevent the Court from functioning as a forum for property speculation and profiteering. By 1859 a total of 3,000 estates worth £21 million had been obtained by 7,489 investors taking advantage of the misfortune of their peers. Most were Irish and the anticipated and hoped for inrush of English landlords with much needed investment capital did not occur. New

proprietors, mindful of the financial travails of the original owners and lacking legal or personal obligations to existing tenants, were frequently less than benign in their actions. Within a few years it was evident that a transformation of the Irish economy was underway. Those who survived on the land, furthermore, looked to the Tenant Protection Society, later the Tenant League, to organise legal opposition to landlord excesses from 1849.[139]

Long term out workings of Famine era 'reforms' encompassed the Fenian sponsored 'Land War' and a series of historic Land Acts in the 1870s and 1880s. Michael Davitt, born in Straide, Mayo, in 1846, was heavily committed to advancing such interests. Davitt's father migrated to England in the summer of 1849 in a final gambit to obtain rent money, but his takings were insufficient to avoid the eviction of the family by Lord Lucan's agents in 1850. Four years before the debacle of the Light Brigade in the Crimea, Lucan's rough handling of his Castlebar estate earned him the sobriquet of 'the old exterminator'.[140] In adulthood Michael Davitt reflected: 'I have a distinct remembrance (doubtless strengthened by the frequent narration of the event by my parents in after years) of that morning's scene: the remnant of our household furniture flung about the road; the roof of the house falling in and the thatch taking fire; my mother [Catherine] and father [Martin] looking on with four young children, the youngest only two months old, adding their cries to the other pangs which must have agitated their souls at the sight of their burning homestead'. Catherine Davitt could not face the destruction of the family unit in Swinford Workhouse and chose instead the travails of the emigrant route to Lancashire, England. Her son returned to Ireland where he fused republican and agrarian activism with great effect.[141]

10. HORROR

By 1849 the worst of the Famine had passed. While conditions had visibly improved in many sectors, this was due in no small part to the terrifying severity of 1847-8. The cottiers and 'spalpeens' were already dead, emigrated or enduring the demeaning regime of the workhouses. 'Asiatic cholera' began to diminish in virulence from mid-1849 while the incidence of smallpox suddenly tripled for unknown reasons. The potato crop, still a vital element, began to recover some of its pre-Famine yield, albeit unevenly and without its former vigour. Even so, scenes of horror were available to anyone in search of them in 1849. Spencer Hall published details of his Famine experiences that year in *Life and Death in Ireland* which recounted his chance meeting with Connor McInerney in a country laneway. McInerney 'had crawled from the workhouse in Limerick' and informed Hall that he wanted to die in the open air as his wife had succumbed in the workhouse and 'his two children would soon be gone too'.[142] Such tragedies were not uncommon in 1849-50, even if their emotional impact on the reading public was dulled by a process of inurement.

Relief advocates were obliged to persevere with appeals given the oft-stated view of British administrators that the Famine had ended. While few were dying in Dublin and Belfast in late 1849, the western counties had not recovered. In May 1849 the *Times* reprinted a series of letters written to Prime Minister Russell from a Church of Ireland Minister in Ballinrobe, Mayo. One related how a man living in a neighbouring Union had cannibalised the heart and liver of a shipwrecked body to feed 'his perishing family'.

Closer to home, the Minister knew of a young woman who had carried the body of her mother on her back into Ballinrobe in the hope of obtaining a coffin only to contract cholera and die within a day of arrival. He reported that 'thousands [are] already lost … [and] people dropping dead of utter want all around in every direction, night and day … It is a burning shame and stain upon the legislature in any so-called Christian country'.[143] Michael O'Shaughnessy, Assistant Barrister of Mayo, was startled by the conditions he encountered when travelling the quarter sessions circuit in April 1849: 'In going from one town to another, it was quite afflicting to see the state of the children; they were nearly naked, with a few rags upon them, the hair standing on an end from poverty; their eyes sunken, their lips pallid, and nothing but the protruding bones of their little joints visible. I could not help exclaiming as I have passed them, "Am I living in a civilised country and part of the British empire?"'[144]

With surreal mistiming, Queen Victoria made her first visit to Ireland in early August 1849 where nothing changed in consequence other than the name of Cobh, County Cork, to Queenstown. It was understood in London that the entourage would not see 'the dark side of Ireland', but being 'not ignorant of these things', Victoria hoped to encourage British investors.[145] It was difficult to reconcile the stated objective of the mission with its itinerary as it was inherently unlikely that British mercantilism could or would seek to operate on the basis that the Famine was present but unseen. Indeed, the royal trip had been mooted on entirely different reasons in 1846 when the deepening food supply crisis suggested postponement. Matters had not greatly improved for the survivors. In July 1849 the Poor Law supported over a million persons, three quarters

of whom were in receipt of outdoor relief. To avoid such unpleasantness the short royal tour was essentially a yachting expedition in which state engagements in Dublin and its more salubrious environs were sandwiched between very brief sojourns in Cobh and Belfast. Road travel through the midlands was out of the question as it would have brought the tourists within sight of the wretched poor.[146]

In a well reported incident, the bands of the 1st Foot and 6th Dragoon Guards played royalist tunes in the Duke of Leinster's Carton Estate, Kildare, before 'dejeuner' was served. Afterwards Victoria evidently enjoyed the 'genuine Irish jig' danced by the teetotaler followers of Fr Theobald Mathew who, whatever their personal achievements, were amongst the least representative examples of the nation's poor.[147] Most of their countrymen would have rated the acquisition of shelter, food and paid work above the pursuit of temperance. The welcome was far from universal and the reinforcement of city garrisons provided evidence of security concerns. On the eve of Victoria's first trip to Dublin the republican ire of Elizabeth Devoy was raised on sighting festive decorations on Sackville (now O'Connell) Street. Her seven-year-old son John recalled how she 'turned away in disgust at the blaze of illuminations'. Within days of this silent protest her eldest son James Devoy, just fourteen, succumbed to the cholera epidemic in Dublin and was buried in Glasnevin. John Devoy survived to become one of the foremost Fenians.[148]

The visit coincided with the publication of news that the annual potato crops of Armagh, Tyrone, Down and other parts of the country were still afflicted by blight. Given this dismal context it is not surprising that the monarch did not, in the interim, endear herself to Irish affections. Another

year of struggle, starvation and disease was promised as the 'Famine Queen' returned to her English palaces.

Hunger forced people to eat whatever could be found locally and the many exigent aberrations which ensued made a strong imprint on the folk record of the survivors. These include accounts of people killing dogs for soup in Rathbawn, County Wicklow, where snails, disinterred animal carcasses, laurel berries and wild mushrooms were gathered for food. It was claimed: 'people mixed cattle blood, mushrooms and cabbage and baked it. They called it relish cakes. They also made wine from elderberries and in frosty weather they ate ice'. Frogs and rats were allegedly and probably fried and eaten in Aughrim, County Wicklow, when the local river was made barren of its fish, eels and grubs. Blackberries were reputedly fought over and nuts consumed in nearby Rednagh by those with the strength to climb trees. Nettles, clover, wild carrot and heather blossoms were eaten further west in Rossport, County Mayo. Once plentiful mountain goats 'were practically wiped out for food' in the Famine-stricken county. Turnips, as with all other root crops and edible plants, were added to Indian Meal during the boiling process to make a more palatable and thicker soup. The fish of Lough Neagh were harvested on an unprecedented scale to augment the diet of East Tyrone natives and benefit those who came into the Coalisland area to obtain sustenance. In coastal counties, such as Sligo and Donegal, seaweed, cockles, barnacles, fluke and sea birds were available.[149]

Stories of theft and its generally harsh judicial consequences were vividly recalled by Famine survivors and their immediate descendants. Brigid Butler of Kilcock, County Kildare, claimed: 'If caught stealing food they were threatened with shooting or transportation to Van Diemen's

Land. There were people named Chandler living in Capagh ... who were caught stealing a bag of potatoes. One of the family was hanged out of a cart on Chandler's Hill and some of the family were transported'.[150] Regardless of the precision of memories seared by trauma, increasing numbers of Irish men, women and children were certainly transported to the penal colonies of New South Wales and Van Diemen's Land during the Famine. Whereas the pre-1845 rate in Ireland averaged 673 sentences per year, some 2,698 received terms of convict exile between August 1847 and August 1848. Clearly, there was a massive increase in the incidence of transportable offenses and a willingness of courts to deport offenders to Australia.[151]

Irish convicts, whether recidivist or novice, were well represented in the last phase of penal transportation to Australia. Fortunately for those embarked, agitation by the Anti-Transportation League in the colonies ensured that the convict system was not only being liberalised but dismantled. Few endured the calculated severity of the 1830s and many received the 'tickets of leave' upon arrival which permitted independent employment under a form of parole. The days of close confinement, sensory deprivation, hard labour and corporal punishment were gone, as were the hard core and recidivist criminals the Port Arthur prison complex had been designed to control.

The implosion of social norms is also reflected in official reports of crime outside Dublin city. Every listed category increased between 1845 and 1851 with the sole exception of sexual assault which declined by more than half. Burglary jumped from ninety-seven known cases in 1845 to 269 in 1846 and it must be assumed that huge numbers of crimes went unreported in the chaos. Overall, 1847 was officially the most challenging Famine year for law

enforcement in rural Ireland when 559 robberies, 561 burglaries, 145 killings and 1,223 instances of livestock theft were recorded. Again, many known but technically undocumented instances of poaching were not enumerated by the constabulary. While robberies increased to 588 cases in 1848, the 1847 figures were otherwise the high watermark of serious crime during the Famine. In crude terms, there were 8,000 crimes of all types reported outside Dublin in 1845 and some 20,000 in 1847. This suggests a correlation between acute social distress and criminal acts, a reading which indicates that law abiding persons were being driven to illegality by extremity.[152] It was also apparent that fewer agrarian 'outrages' were taking place, presumably owing to the collapse of the social cohesion and common purpose necessary to commit large scale Whiteboy/Ribbon-style demonstrations. Sir John Vandeleur Stewart informed a Select Committee on the Irish Poor Laws in May 1849 that 'what are ordinarily called agrarian crimes have diminished'.[153]

Wicklow magistrate Bartholomew Warburton divined from the calendar of Tinahely's summer quarter sessions of 1849 that many crimes of larceny had been committed by persons inside workhouses who desired the better food available in the county goal. Others who came before the Tinahely court had deliberately sought imprisonment as a survival strategy after being denied admission to the workhouses. Persons jailed and transported for criminality were guaranteed food, shelter and clothing, by no means inconsiderable attractions to the desperate.[154] O'Shaughnessy, the Mayo barrister, noted a series of 'distressing instances ... of persons desiring to be transported' at the Westport assizes in April 1849. These included youths Martin McGunty, John McGrene and John English who were convicted of stealing

hemp. O'Shaughnessy recalled 'they were each about 17 years of age; they requested to be transported, as they had no means of living, and must do the same thing again'. Michael Eady, similarly, asked to be sent to Australia, while his eighteen-year-old brother Owen, a defendant in a different case, 'said he should rob again if let out'. The barrister enquired 'if he knew what transportation was' to which Eady replied 'he knew he would be kept at work for seven years, and that at the end he would have liberty in another country, which would be better than starving, and sleeping out at night'. Margaret Heston and Mary Walsh, 'two young girls', denied understanding the punishment they requested, but insisted they had taken two heifers 'to get into gaol and be transported' and that 'anything was better than hunger'.[155]

The Antipodes, however, were increasingly the destination of voluntary migrants availing of estate clearances and government sponsored 'assisted passage' schemes which made the expensive trip economically viable. The Irish were needed in the white settler dominions of the Empire and a special group of several thousand female Famine orphans were sent to Australia in 1848. Although initially denied welcome, the orphan girls soon proved very popular in a colony in need of female settlers. In all, 53,801 Irish migrants went to the Australia and New Zealand as free settlers between 1851 and 1855.[156] Demand was known to have been high during the early years of the Famine when the Guardians of Mallow Union 'were very anxious to send out females'. The programme was suspended when 'young women who were in service ... Flocked into the [work]house in order to be put upon the emigration list'.[157]

11. AN GHORTA MÓR, THE IRISH HOLOCAUST

Having peaked with appalling consequences in 1847-8, the Great Famine eventually began to show signs of waning in 1850-51. Many areas had emerged from the crisis somewhat earlier and few counties or regions underwent exactly comparable privations. Partial recovery of the potato crop was obviously a contributory factor in national recovery and one which sustained those either unwilling or unable to contemplate immediate emigration. Workhouse dependency also gradually slowed the excess mortality rate. Occupancy of workhouses remained extremely high by the standards of the United Kingdom, notwithstanding the many factors inhibiting entry. The centrality of the Poor Law system in 1850 can be gauged from the fact that over 46,000 persons died in workhouses that year. Regional differences remained with Roscommon, Mayo and Galway being particularly slow to stabilise.[158]

John Wallace, a resident of Kanturk Union workhouse, wrote to his uncles in America in September 1850 seeking assistance on behalf of his Cork relatives. The family was by no means destitute, owning a vacant riverside farm of forty acres and a degree of influence in clerical appointments. Those obliged to enter Kanturk workhouse, however, faced an uncertain future if such assets could not be readily exploited as the Famine retreated. Wallace asserted: 'often have I pondered in gloomy silence over the scenes here before me, and contrasted them with the accounts you sent us from America. How often I looked upon crowded hospitals and workhouse walls crowded to suffocation, the heart-shaking pleading of the children deprived of their

parents, separated perhaps never to meet again until their bodies may meet in the charmed house of their souls in heaven. Oh, if I could make you one-half sensible of the state of things in this country you would raise your eyes to heaven, strike your breast and thank the Almighty for that inspiration that first prompted you to leave this unhappy land of your nativity. A land of craft, deceit, and treachery, a land of poverty and mendicancy, teeming now only with pauperised inhabitants, tax collectors, workhouses and Hospitals'. John Wallace, a man of some means, was instrumental in arranging the migration of several relatives to Jackson County, Iowa, from 'this Island of sorrow and poverty'.[159]

The precise number of Famine dead in Ireland will never be known owing to the inability of Government to derive an accurate census from their enquiries in 1841. Given the scale of the challenge, it is not surprising that state agencies also failed to compile accurate figures of the dead and emigrated. By 1851, however, eleven of the thirty-two counties had lost in excess of 23 per cent of their officially registered pre-Famine population. A conservative estimate by economic historian Joel Mokyr puts the minimum national excess death toll of 1846-51 at a staggering 1,082,000. This total excludes the approximately 50,000 deaths of people during flight abroad and immediately following arrival. This makes no allowance for lack of natural increase in Ireland due to the twin determinants of premature death and permanent relocation abroad. Mayo, Sligo, Roscommon, Galway, Leitrim and Cavan suffered annual excess mortality in the range of 42-58 persons per 1,000 in 1846-51 with Cork, Clare, Fermanagh, Monaghan, Tipperary, Kerry, Queen's County (Laois), Waterford, Longford and Westmeath all falling within the 20-32 per thousand

range. Two major trends were manifested: 40 per cent of all deaths occurred in Connacht and 30 per cent in Munster. Ulster, where almost 21 per cent of deaths took place, was particularly hard hit in the southern part of the province where Fermanagh and Cavan were markedly more deadly than Tyrone and Armagh.[160]

Dublin proved a statistical anomaly as the metropolitan and county populations actually recorded a small positive increase despite thousands of Famine-related deaths taking place inside its boundaries. This may be explained, in part, by the comparative lack of potato dependence and a more convenient and effective relief structure than elsewhere. Also, the movement of persons into the city environs for the purposes of assistance, medical treatment and embarkation from the port clearly distorted the picture. Over a fifth of the surviving Wicklow-born population had resettled in Dublin by 1851.[161] Belfast simultaneously attracted Antrim-, Down-, Tyrone- and Fermanagh-born migrants, and small numbers from further afield. Limerick was similarly anomalous with an excess death rate of only ten per thousand per annum, which contrasted very favourably with the high levels of mortality in contiguous counties Tipperary, Clare and Kerry. However, 67,897 Limerick residents either died within, or had emigrated beyond, the county borders by 1851. The sector was far from unscathed. At the same time, the population of Limerick city, and its North Liberties in particular, rose by 8,291 from the 1841 census to a new total 57,854 in 1851.[162] The district was evidently a convenient and receptive refuge, an example of rural famine prompting urbanisation in north Munster. Donegal fared surprisingly well under the circumstances and, if parts of the county suffered heavily, the total excess loss of 10.7 people per thousand per year was comparatively few. This may

reflect greater access to maritime resources such as fish and seaweed, as well as geographic isolation from communicative diseases.[163]

Emigration from Ireland continued at rates rarely recorded in international history in terms of both actual numbers and per capita outflow. In 1848, the year following the 'coffin ship' sensation, at least 181,361 elected to take their chances by departing Ireland. Evictions and the warped economics of 'Rate-in-Aid' drove 218,842 overseas in 1849 and another 213,616 in 1850. Between 1851 and 1852, when available food supply relegated starvation and disease from the status of mass killers, 254,537 and 368,746, persons left respectively. While excess mortality rates declined sharply, the demographic tidal wave of depopulation continued in post-Famine Ireland. The prospect of life and progress in the shattered countryside in 1853 was shunned by the 192,609 people who left that year, as well as by the 150,209 who followed in 1854. By then it was inherently unlikely that Ireland would ever resemble the country it had been just nine years earlier.[164]

Recent scholarship has highlighted the relationship between death rates and three key elements; household income, farm size and literacy. These factors were generally more important than the mere presence of blight in determining who lived and who died. In short, areas with the lowest per capita income, highest concentrations of small holdings and highest illiteracy rates were significantly more likely to suffer excess mortality. Poverty, therefore, was a major contributor to death rates, an obvious verdict in a country where persons with the cash to buy food survived unless killed by the indiscriminate ravages of infectious disease.

The Irish Poor Law, an inferior version of the English original, was designed to contain vagrancy and other manifestations of economic distress but was incapable of addressing its myriad causes. Its implementation illustrated how the Imperial mode of government was consistently less efficient than the subordinate colonial forum abolished at the turn of the century. Long-term state underinvestment and a culture of administrative neglect ensured that Irish living standards had declined to the point that they were insufficient to safeguard the survival of a major bloc of the population when blight triggered a social catastrophe in 1845-6. Standard relief measures and minor short term interventions authorised by London were found to be helpful, at best, rather than decisive. A second year of blight infestation, however, confounded British civil servants who believed that limited and inexpensive state intervention would suffice in lieu of responsible Government. As 1847 progressed, the persistent refusal of central government to finance, empower and organise its detached Irish relief administration doomed the first thousands of a million fatalities. After the ascendancy of the Whigs in 1846, the rigid theorems of *laissez-faire* failed every short term economic policy to which it was applied with calamitous results.

Public works, an imaginative and bold scheme capable of providing wages for much needed infrastructural projects, proved politically untenable owing the perceived costs and its allegedly disruptive nature. Soup kitchens, when operated as private and state-backed enterprises, were also successful until prematurely phased out. 'Rate-in--Aid', coupled with a series of utterly misguided Treasury inspired strictures, added to the increasingly confused and contradictory attitude of the Executive towards Ireland.

Issues of fiscal responsibility at the height of an unprecedented Famine crisis indicated that Ireland's membership of the United Kingdom masked its true status as a problematic colony. The special treatment provided to blight threatened Scotland and controversial management of the grain trade further highlighted the fiction of Union. Three Famine Viceroys encountered opposition in Westminster when attempting to exercise the duties of their office, as did several other key administrative personnel. The crudest propaganda of the Repeal movement and Young Ireland appeared to be all too credible in the light of such wrangling.

The mid-term effects of the Great Famine were considerable and reverberated strongly throughout the century. Emigration continued in dimensions which resulted in dramatic changes to land tenure, utilisation and farm size. British administrators became somewhat more responsive to the intricacies of Irish agrarian issues and more wary of the consequences of their past incompetence. Irish politicians gradually re-coalesced in Westminster and articulated their positions with greater organisational ability and collective force than before. From the 1850s the constitutionalists vied with an underground alternate stream which, aided by the resurgent diaspora in North America, agitated for a revolutionary solution. In 1881 Davitt described this phenomena as 'the wolfdog of Irish vengeance', one of the forces which inspired Devoy, O'Donovan Rossa and countless others.[165] The Irish Republican Brotherhood and Fenians derived their potency from the post-Famine anger of expatriates, allied to that of survivors in Ireland. Major John McBride, when recruiting Irishmen to fight the British army in South Africa in 1899 exhorted a Johannesburg crowd to oppose 'the Empire of the gibbet and the pitchcap, of the famine

graves and the coffin ships, of the battering ram and the convict cell'. McBride was executed for his role in the 1916 Rising which in turn spawned the War of Independence.[166]

The Great Famine dealt Ireland a profound physical and psychological shock, which altered the course of the nation's history to an extent that defies conventional narrative relation.

ENDNOTES

1. Cited in *Irish Echo*, 5 August 1997.
2. W.E. Vaughan and A.J. Fitzpatrick (eds.), *Irish Historical Statistics, Population, 1821-1971* (Dublin, 1978), p. 3.
3. Liam Kennedy, Paul Ell, E.M. Crawford and L.A. Clarkson, *Mapping the Great Irish Famine* (Dublin, 1999), p. 26.
4. James S. Donnelly Jr, *The Great Irish potato Famine* (Stroud, 2001), p. 178.
5. Sean Duffy (ed) *Atlas of Irish History* (Dublin, 1997), p. 88.
6. F.H.A. Aalen, Kevin Whelan and Mathew Stout (eds.) *Atlas of the Irish rural landscape* (Cork, 1997), pp. 82-91, 190-92.
7. See Austin Bourke, *'The visitation of God'? The potato and the great Irish famine* (Dublin, 1993), pp. 32-9.
8. Peter Beresford Ellis, *Eyewitness to Irish History* (New Jersey, 2004), p. 170 and Aalen, Whelan and Stout (eds.), *Atlas*, p. 87.
9. David Dickson, *Arctic Ireland, The extraordinary story of the Great Frost and Forgotten Famine of 1740-41* (Belfast, 1997) and Christine Kinealy, *A death-dealing Famine, The Great Hunger in Ireland* (London, 1997), pp. 42-7.
10. For the north east see Martin W. Dowling, *Tenant Right and Agrarian Society in Ulster, 1600-1870* (Dublin, 1999), chapter four.
11. See Cormac O Grada, *Ireland, A new economic history, 1780-1939* (Oxford, 1994), chapter four and L.A. Clarkson and E. Margaret Crawford, *Feast and Famine, A history of food and nutrition in Ireland 1500-1920* (Oxford, 2001), chapter four.
12. Aalen et al (eds.), *Atlas*, pp. 84-6, 88-9.
13. Nassau Senior, *Letter from Nassau W. Senior, Esq, to His Majesty's Principal Secretary of State for the Home Department, on the Third Report from the Commissioners for Inquiring into the condition of the poor in Ireland, dated 14 April 1836* (London, 1837), pp. 4-5.
14. Senior, *Letter from Nassau W. Senior*, pp. 5-6.
15. Jacinta Prunty, *Dublin slums, 1800-1925, a study in urban geography* (Dublin, 1998), chapter six.
16. John O'Connor, *The Workhouses of Ireland, the fate of Ireland's poor* (Dublin, 1995), p. 68.
17. O'Connor, *Workhouses*, pp.88-9 and Kennedy et al, *Mapping*, p. 18.
18. Bourke, *Visitation of God*, pp. 30-32.
19. John Percivil, *The Great Famine, Ireland's potato famine, 1845-51* (London, 1995), p. 55.
20. *Dublin Evening Post*, 9 September 1845.
21. Donnelly, *Famine*, pp. 44-6 and Christine Kinealy, *Death-dealing Famine*, pp. 52-9.
22. Bourke, *Visitation of God*, pp. 140-49.
23. See 'Advice concerning the potato crop to the farmers and peasantry of Ireland' in *Downpatrick Recorder*, 8 November 1845 and John Killen (ed.), *The Famine decade, contemporary accounts, 1841-1851* (Belfast, 1995), pp.

38-40.

24.   *A return of the highest price of potatoes in the various market towns in Ireland ... for the last seven years* (London, 1846), p. 1.

25.   See *Illustrated London News*, 18 October 1845.

26.   See Alice M. De Jarnett, 'The Irish potato Famine fungus, Phytophthora infestans (Mont.) de Bary', *Southern Illinois University, Carbondale, Ehthnobotanical leaflets* (Carbondale, 1999).

27.   See Peter Gray, *Famine, land and politics, British Government and Irish Society, 1843-50* (Dublin, 1999) and Maurice O'Connell, *Daniel O'Connell, The man and his politics* (Dublin, 1990).

28.   Brendan O Cathaoir (ed.), *Famine Diary* (Dublin, 1999), p. 6.

29.   *Times*, 14 February 1846.

30.   Minutes of the North Dublin Union, 17 December 1845 cited in Prunty, *Dublin slums*, p. 228.

31.   See Richard Davis, *Revolutionary Imperialist, William Smith O'Brien, 1803-1864* (Dublin, 1998), p. 131.

32.   For the Emancipation campaign see Oliver MacDonagh, *The hereditary bondsman, Daniel O'Connell, 1775-1829* (London, 1988).

33.   Donnelly, *Famine*, p. 38.

34.   See O'Cathaoir, *Famine Diary*, pp. 10-12.

35.   *Extract of a Report of the Commissioners of Inquiry into matters connected with the failure of the Potato Crop* (London, 1846).

36.   See Mansion House Committee resolutions in Killen (ed.) *Famine Decade*, p. 43.

37.   For traditions of 'Indian Corn' see Cathal Poirteir (ed.), *Famine Echoes* (Dublin, 1995), chapter nine and *Illustrated London News*, 4 April 1846.

38.   Quoted in Bourke, *Visitation of God*, p. 163.

39.   Dunkellon Barony Petition to Heytesbury, 13 April 1846 quoted in Colm Tobin and Diarmaid Ferriter (eds.), *The Irish Famine, a documentary*, U.S. edn. (New York, 2002) p. 64.

40.   See *Abstracts of the most serious representations made by the several Medical Superintendents of Public Institutions ... 1846* (London, 1846).

41.   Donnelly, *Famine*, pp. 76-80.

42.   *Times*, 11 January 1847.

43.   See Sixteenth annual report of the Commissioners of Public Works, Dublin, 1848 in Killen (ed.) *Famine Decade*, pp. 166-8.

44.   *Report of the Commissioners of Inquiry ... 1846*, p. 2.

45.   Quoted in O'Cathaoir, *Famine Diary*, p. 65.

46.   Russell to Duke of Leinster, 17 October 1846 (http://www.swan.ac.uk/history/teaching/teaching resources/An Gorta Mor).

47.   See Jim Rees, *Surplus people, The Fitzwilliam clearances, 1847-1856* (Cork, 2000), p. 33.

48.   *Representations made by the several Medical Superintendents ... 1846*, p. 2.

49.   Quoted in Tom Hayden, *Irish on the inside, In search of the soul of Irish America* (London, 2001), p. 14.

50.   See Gray, *Famine*.

51.   See Christine Kinealy, 'The evidence of the Great Famine' in Terrence

McDonough (ed.) *Was Ireland a colony? Economics, politics and culture in Nineteenth-Century Ireland* (Dublin, 2005), pp. 52-3.

52.   Bourke, *Visitation of God*, p. 168.

53.   Routh to Trevelyan, 29 September 1846 cited in Bourke, *Visitation of God*, p. 164.

54.   Russell to Duke of Leinster, 17 October 1846 (http://www.swan.ac.uk/history/teaching/teaching_resources/An Gorta Mor). See also Gray, *Famine*, p. 118.

55.   Bourke, *Visitation of God*, p. 167.

56.   *An account "of all cattle, sheep and swine imported into Great Britain from Ireland from the 10 day of October 1845 to the 5 day of January 1846"* (London, 1846).

57.   Sean Spellissy, *The history of Limerick city* (Limerick, 1998), p. 70.

58.   O'Cathaoir, *Famine Diary*, p. 25.

59.   Government Official, 24 April 1846 cited in Beresford Ellis, *Eyewitness*, p. 171.

60.   *Cork Examiner*, 4 September 1846.

61.   *Cork Examiner*, 23 September 1846.

62.   *Cork Examiner*, 18 September 1846.

63.   Proclamation, 2 October 1846 cited in Tobin and Ferriter (eds.) *Famine*, p. 82.

64.   *Illustrated London News*, 7 November 1846.

65.   *Cork Examiner*, 30 October 1846.

66.   *Kerry Examiner* and *Mayo Constitution* cited in *Cork Examiner*, 23 November 1846.

67.   *Cork Examiner*, 1 January 1847.

68.   *Cork Examiner*, 4 December 1846.

69.   James Crosfield, *Distress in Ireland* (Dublin, 1847) cited in O'Connor, *Workhouses*, pp. 126-7.

70.   Wynne to Harry Jones, 24 December 1846 cited in O'Connor, *Workhouses*, pp. 128-9.

71.   Terry Golway, *Irish rebel, John Devoy and America's fight for Ireland's freedom* (New York, 1999), pp. 28-9.

72.   *Cork Examiner*, 6 January 1847. See also Patrick Hickey, 'The Famine in Skibbereen Union (1845-51) in Cathal Poirteir (ed.) *The Great Irish Famine* (Cork, 1995), pp. 185-203.

73.   *Cork Examiner*, 18 January 1847.

74.   *Cork Examiner*, 22 January 1847.

75.   *Times*, 11 January 1847.

76.   *Times*, 11 January 1847.

77.   Lord Dufferin and G.G. Boyle, *Narrative of a journey from Oxford to Skibbereen during the year of the Irish Famine*, 3 edn. (Oxford, 1847).

78.   Cited in Killen (ed.), *Famine Decade*, pp. 130-31.

79.   O'Cathaoir, *Famine Diary*, pp. 102, 107 and Christine Kinealy and Gerard MacAtasney, *The Hidden Famine, Hunger, poverty and sectarianism in Belfast, 1840-50* (London, 2000), pp. 95-6. See also Tom Hartley, *Written in Stone, The History of Belfast City Cemetery* (Belfast, 2006), pp. 15-16.

80.   Gray, *Famine*, pp. 262-5.

81.   *Cork Examiner*, 9 November 1846.

82. Donnelly, *Famine*, p. 83.

83. Rees, *Surplus people*, pp. 61-2.

84. Donnelly, *Famine*, pp. 179-85.

85. Rees, *Surplus people*, p. 127.

86. Rees, *Surplus people*, p. 80.

87. Donnelly, *Famine*, p. 181.

88. Robert Sellar, *The Summer of Sorrow* (Quebec, 1895) cited in Beresford Ellis, *Eyewitness*

89. Sellar cited in Ellis, *Eyewitness*, p. 177.

90. Donald Akenson, *The Irish diaspora, a primer* (Belfast, 1996), p. 198 and Donnelly, *Famine*, p. 178.

91. *Report of the Commissioners of Inquiry … 1846*, pp. 1-2.

92. Prunty, *Dublin slums*, pp. 227-33.

93. See Prunty, *Slums*, p. 229.

94. See Laurence M. Geary, 'Famine, fever and the bloody flux' in Poirteir (ed.) *Great Irish Famine*, pp. 74-85 and Kennedy et al (eds.) *Mapping*, pp. 104-24.

95. Fr. Henry Brennan to the editor, *Weekly Freeman's Journal*, 17 July 1847.

96. James Hack Tuke, *A visit to Connaught in the autumn of 1847. A letter addressed to the Central Relief Committee of the Society of Friends* (London, 1847).

97. *Nation*, 3 March 1847, *Cork Examiner*, 23 July 1847 and Kinealy, *Death-dealing Famine*, pp. 114-7.

98. See Kinealy and MacAtasney, *Hidden Famine*, p. 114.

99. *Cork Examiner*, 1 January 1847.

100. See Christine Kinealy, 'Potatoes, politics and philanthropy: The role of private charity during the Irish Famine' in Patrick O'Sullivan (ed.) *The meaning of the Famine* (London, 1997), pp. 140-171.

101. Michael Davitt, *Jottings in Solitary*, new edn. (Dublin, 2004), p. 194.

102. *Nation*, 12 June 1847.

103. *British Parliamentary Papers (8) Reports of the Relief Commissioners, 1846-53*, p. 23 cited in Tobin and Ferriter (eds.) *Famine*, p. 184. See also Donnelly, *Famine*, pp. 62-3.

104. *Cork Examiner*, 25 October 1847.

105. O'Cathaoir, *Famine Diary*, p. 108.

106. See Davis, *Smith O'Brien*, pp. 193-223.

107. *Nation*, 6 November 1847.

108. See Donnelly, *Famine*, pp. 142-3.

109. O'Cathaoir *Famine Diary*, p. 150.

110. See O'Cathaoir, *Famine Diary*, pp. 150-51.

111. For figures given by Lord Gort in House of Lords in 1832 see D.J. Hickey and J.E. Doherty, *A Dictionary of Irish history, 1800-1980* (Dublin, 1987), p. 561.

112. See Donnelly, *Famine*, p. 8.

113. Gray, *Famine*, pp. 53-4, 192.

114. See Charles Trevelyan, *The Irish Crisis*, (London, 1848).

115. See Kinealy, *Death-dealing Famine*, pp. 123-4.

116. *Tipperary Vindicator* quoted in *Illustrated London News*, 16 December 1848.

117. See Clarkson and Crawford, *Feast and Famine*, pp. 158-60.

118. John M. Hearne, 'Thomas Francis Meagher: Reluctant Revolutionary' in Hearne and Cornish (eds.) *Meagher*, p. 82.
119. Quoted in Thomas Kenneally, The *Great Shame, A story of the Irish in the old world and the new* (London, 1998), p. 154.
120. Meagher quoted in Hearne and Cornish (eds.), *Meagher*, p. 86.
121. See *Times*, 4 October 1848.
122. Cited in Gray, *Famine*
123. O'Connor, *Workhouses*, p. 123.
124. O'Connor, *Workhouses*, p. 140.
125. *Cork Examiner*, 12 December 1847.
126. Prunty, *Dublin slums*, p. 229.
127. See O'Connor, *Workhouses*, Appendix 13, pp. 259-64.
128. O'Connor, *Workhouses*, p. 142.'
129. Quoted in Donnelly, *Famine*, p. 26.
130. O'Cathaoir, *Famine Diary*, p. 166.
131. *Dublin University Magazine*, XXIX, April 1847, p. 514 cited in Tobin and Ferriter (eds.) *Famine*, p. 185.
132. Kinnealy and MacAtasney, *Hidden Famine*, p. 159.
133. See R.K. Engen (ed.) *Dictionary of Victorian Wood Engravers* (Cambridge, 1985).
134. Senior, *Letter from Nassau W. Senior*, pp. 4-5.
135. See Gray, *Famine*, pp. 280-81.
136. Donnelly, *Famine*, pp. 138-40.
137. See *Illustrated London News*, 15 December 1849.
138. *Report of the Select Committee appointed on the Irish Poor Law ... May 1849* (London, 1849), pp. 10-11.
139. See Kinealy, *Death- dealing Famine*, pp. 140-1.
140. See T. W. Moody, *Davitt and Irish Revolution, 1846-82* (Oxford, 1981), pp. 3-8.
141. Cited in Moody, *Davitt*, pp. 8-9.
142. Cited in O'Connor, *Workhouses*, p. 151.
143. *Times*, 23 May 1849.
144. *Report of the Select Committee ... 1849*, p. 40.
145. *Illustrated London News*, 4 August 1849.
146. Kinealy, *Death dealing Famine*, p. 137.
147. *Illustrated London News*, 4 August 1849.
148. Cited in Golway, *Irish Rebel*, p. 117. See also Ibid., pp. 32-3.
149. Poirteir (ed.), *Famine Echoes*, pp. 54-7, 61-3.
150. Quoted in Porteir (ed.), *Famine Echoes*, p. 79.
151. A.G.L. Shaw, *Convicts and the Colonies, A study of penal transportation form Great Britain and Ireland to Australia and other parts of the British Empire* (London, 1966), p. 338.
152. See Cormac O'Grada, *Ireland: A New Economic History, 1780-1939* (Oxford, 1994), p. 203.
153. *Report of the Select Committee ... 1849*, p. 2.
154. Ken Hannigan, 'Wicklow before and after the Famine' in Ken Hannigan and William Nolan (eds.) *Wicklow, History and Society* (Dublin, 1994), p. 809.

155. *Report of the Select Committee … 1849*, p. 39.
156. *Commission on emigration and other population problems* (Dublin, 1954), pp. 309-11 cited in Tobin and Ferriter (eds.) *Famine*, p. 171. See also 'Return of the orphan girls sent out from workhouses in Ireland, as emigrants to Australia … 1848' in O'Connor, *Workhouses*, pp. 257-8.
157. *Report of the Select Committee … 1849*, p. 25.
158. O'Grada, *Ireland*, p. 177.
159. John C. Wallace to his uncles, 6 September 1850 (Private Collection, Wallace family, Chicago, Illinois).
160. Joel Mokyr, *Why Ireland starved: A quantitative and analytical history of the Irish economy, 1800-1850* (London, second edition, 1985), pp. 266-7 and Donnelly, *Famine*, pp. 176-8.
161. Rees, *Surplus people*, p. iv.
162. See evidence of Denis O'Connor in *Report of the Select Committee … 1849*, pp. 50-54.
163. Spellissy, *Limerick*, p. 233.
164. Fitzpatrick, *Irish Emigration*, p. 4. See also *Illustrated London News*, 6 July 1850.
165. Quoted in Moody, *Davitt*, p. 449.
166. *United Irishman*, 25 November 1899.

Acknowledgements

Thanks to John Logan, Ciara Breathnach, Owen Rodgers, David Fleming and Helen Carr.